Civic Learning
and Teaching

Civic Learning
and Teaching

Edited by Ashley Finley
Bringing Theory to Practice
Washington, DC

1818 R Street NW, Washington, DC 20009

ISBN 978-0-9853088-5-8

Civic Learning and Teaching

A Bridge to Civic Life and a Life of Learning

EDITOR: Ashley Finley

CIVIC SERIES EDITOR: Barry Checkoway

CONTENTS

FOREWORD

What is, or should be, the civic mission of higher education? The Civic Series grew out of the assumption that thoughtful authors sharing their ideas about this question can contribute to institutional change on campus and in the community.

The Civic Seminar Initiative (funded by Bringing Theory to Practice) has complemented this purpose by supporting hundreds of campus seminars in which individuals discussed higher education's civic mission and how to strengthen it at the institutional level. The seminars were based on the notion that when individuals join together for a common cause, they can accomplish more together than any single person can acting alone.

Imagine a university whose purpose is to prepare students for active roles in a democratic society; whose curricula and courses challenge students' imaginations and develop their civic competencies; whose cocurricular activities offer multiple opportunities for students to engage in public work; whose relationships include dialogue and debate about civic theory and practice—and whose faculty and staff members support students at every stage of the process.

Civic Learning and Teaching is a metaphor for a university of this type. From every corner of the campus, its authors are asking provocative questions about the civic:

What is the future of the civic in an online world? What happens when civic learning is viewed in relation to intergroup dialogue, as a form of social justice, or as an approach to activist science or public art? What are some strategies for assessing the outcomes of civic work? What lessons can be taken from best practices, and how can scholars and practitioners use the knowledge gained from these practices to strengthen the institution?

Ashley Finley has produced a volume whose authors are asking such questions about the civic. Is it possible that there are individuals on your own campus who are also asking similar questions? And is it possible that they are asking these questions in isolation but not together—and that, if they were to meet they might become more aware of their common cause and, in so doing, advance the civic mission of your university?

If the chapters of this monograph, itself so much like a university, are used to prepare seminar participants on your own campus, then its purpose—and that of the larger series—will be served.

Barry Checkoway
General Series Editor

ACKNOWLEDGMENTS

In order to gather, assemble, and edit the following pages, I have relied heavily on the goodwill and patience of many people. I am grateful, first, to the authors, whose good thoughts and writing fill the following pages, for taking valuable time away from their busy lives and careers to make these chapters a reality. I owe immeasurable thanks to Kathryn Peltier Campbell whose fine editing and consistent feedback helped maintain an unwaivering commitment to quality in the final product. And because there is always a wizard (or two) behind the curtain who do the truly effortful work of getting a publication to and through press, I must thank Dylan Joyce for his thoughtful stewardship of this process from start to finish and Liz Clark, whose design work has provided invaluable visual appeal cover to cover.

Finally, I want to thank the many hundreds of students who have in one way or another inspired the authors who have contributed to this monograph, who have inspired me as an educator, and who have inspired the practitioners—faculty, staff, and community members—who will use this monograph to continue their own good work. It is because of those students, and the many more to come, that civic learning and teaching enriches higher education and the lives we strive to lead.

Ashley Finley
Editor

ABOUT THE EDITOR

Ashley Finley is national evaluator for Bringing Theory to Practice, as well as senior director of assessment and research at the Association of American Colleges and Universities.

INTRODUCTION
Ashley Finley

Civic Learning and Teaching is not a guide to get students out of the classroom and into the community. It is not a manual for service learning or for community-based research. And although the chapters contain plenty of guidance and practical application, the authors have not neatly laid out the steps of their independent approaches for engaging students civically. Instead, each author has insightfully taken on the task of articulating why civic learning and teaching matters, and why it has the power to transform students, faculty, staff, and—hopefully—communities. This monograph is intended to provide readers with inspiration for new practices, reminders of why they are working so hard to infuse the civic into their own learning spaces, and a new understanding of what it means not just to "do" civic learning and teaching, but to do these things well.

Civic Learning and Teaching was conceived on the notion that effective, truly transformative civic learning and teaching is a means of transcending boundaries, both literal and figurative. At their best, civic practices can permeate the dividing lines between campus and community spaces, whether physical walls or the ether between virtual worlds. The practice of civic learning and teaching does not distinguish between the traditional roles of "student," "teacher," and "community member"; instead, it assumes that everyone is or will be all three, either simultaneously or in turn. Civic learning and teaching does not seek to erase differences between the people who enter into these practices, but rather to prompt participants to acknowledge, explore, and appreciate what their differences mean. In this vein, each contributing author examines some dimension of the liminal nature of civic learning and teaching—these practices that allow us to explore the ambiguity between the spaces we occupy, the roles we serve, and the differences that divide us.

In the first chapter, Dan Butin examines what civic learning and teaching mean today—at this point in the twenty-first century and at this fraught moment for higher education. Butin explores the concept of time through a civic lens by asking how civic learning and teaching provide a means of transitioning from an era where students had the time and space to explore deeply in traditional classroom settings, to a time when learning is increasingly digital and increasingly focused on efficiency. How does a commitment to civic learning and teaching help us maintain quality standards in this changing landscape?

Seth Pollack focuses in chapter two on civic learning and teaching as a means of bridging boundaries across disciplines. Pollack analyzes how California State University–Monterey Bay's approach to civic literacy across the curriculum has helped create shared ownership of the institution's commitment to civic outcomes across a diverse community of faculty and other campus stakeholders. Furthermore, Pollack thoughtfully considers how a focus on civic literacy enables students to integrate and apply knowledge and experiences across an interdisciplinary range of courses, resulting in deeper levels of learning.

In chapter three, Barbara Holland examines civic learning and teaching through an outcomes- and assessment-focused lens. Holland provides a cogent framework for considering how the outcomes of civic practices need not be strictly student-centered or institutionally based, but also can serve the interests of the community partners so often neglected in the assessment process. She offers rich insights into the ingredients needed to develop an approach to assessing civic learning and teaching that is beneficial and engaging across all levels of campus and community partnerships.

In chapter four, Patricia Gurin and Biren (Ratnesh) Nagda engage civic learning and teaching through the lens of intergroup dialogue as a means of bridging differences among learners and as a way of resolving differences encountered in civic exchange. Gurin and Nagda argue that rather than existing as separate experiences with distinct outcomes, intergroup dialogue and service-learning courses can intersect to offer routes toward connecting learning and deepening students' civic understanding and engagement. The examples they provide, contextualized in part through students' reflections, remind us how crucial it is to remember student voices when engaging in civic learning and teaching.

Next, Christina Colon and John Rowden explore in chapter five how the practice of "citizen science" blurs the lines between the roles of scientist and activist. The authors, one of whom is a biology professor and the other a community partner with the New York City Audubon Society, detail what it means for students and community members to work alongside one another while conducting environmental research with significance to community health and well-being. Their work, as authors for this monograph and as campus–community partners in New York City, exemplifies the true spirit of civic learning and teaching: the fostering of meaningful, authentic collaboration.

In chapter six, Sybril Bennett examines the significance of civility in the digital age by asking what it means for students to practice civility in virtual spaces, and how we adjust our definition of and expectations for civility when the consequences of incivility are increasingly distal, intangible, and disconnected. Bennett suggests several contexts for exploring this timely take on civic learning and teaching, including her own innovative course on digital citizenship.

The final chapter, by Carole Frances Lung, is a statement about what civic learning and teaching look like from the perspective of a public artist. Although she offers examples of public art throughout the chapter, Lung's real objective is to reframe (or "retool," in her words) the entire structure of the university, using artistic values and practices to create an educational experience that fosters civic-minded, whole students. Lung's provocation is a full examination of what is needed to create such a "retooled university," its mission, and the terms at its core.

This monograph concludes with an afterword by Timothy Eatman, who provides a bird's-eye look at civic learning and teaching through the perspective of having worked with an array of colleges and universities as co-director of the Imagining America consortium. Eatman's closing is not summative; rather, it is motivational. He implores us to examine for a final time what it means to do civic learning and teaching *well*. To this end, Eatman offers examples of courageous programs across the country on the cutting edge of transformative civic practice. He also provides a framework for developing our "five senses of engagement" to better conceptualize the meaning (and center) of civic practice. In doing so, Eatman nudges us to think critically about the civic efforts we are undertaking—for the sake of our students, ourselves, our institutions, and the communities in which we live and work.

Like the civic practices and ideals that fill the following pages, this monograph is intended to provoke a shared experience. It is meant to be useful, provocative, challenging, and surprising; but the true marker of its success will be the conversations and actions it inspires.

The Future of the Civic in an Online World

Dan Butin

1

HIGHER EDUCATION IS BEING FUNDAMENTALLY DISRUPTED. Within a decade, teaching and learning will be transformed for a huge number of students across a broad swath of colleges and universities due to a wide range of digital learning technologies. This essay is thus an attempt to rethink and begin to grapple with the future of civic learning and teaching in an increasingly online world. Namely, I want to argue that as teaching and learning move further and further into "the cloud," civic learning, as a deeply place-based endeavor, may offer the only remaining coherent vision for the future viability of higher education.

So let me begin with a provocation. Let me suggest that teaching and learning as we know them will soon be no more, that political and fiscal pressures will align with technological advancements and an accruing body of substantive research to promulgate the use of hybrid models of education whereby online and computer-mediated instruction become ever more commonplace in post-secondary education.[1]

That vision is not the provocation. Those are just the facts on the ground. We are already living through those times.[2] The provocation is that this stampeding reality is a good thing because it finally puts to rest the tattered and quaint story-line of college as all about and only good for the "life of the mind." In so doing, it allows us—faculty and administrators committed to the idea of higher education as a public good—to focus on shaping the true value proposition of higher education: that civic learning, in its commitment to pedagogies that link theory and practice within the sphere of the public commons, offers one of the only modes for educating a thoughtful citizenry able to critically engage with the complexities of living in a pluralistic, inequitable, and interconnected world.[3]

LAYING THE GROUNDWORK FOR CIVIC LEARNING IN AN ONLINE WORLD
Like it or not, the monopoly of place-based institutions and their traditional value proposition has been fundamentally shattered. Demographic changes, market pressures, and technological advancements have eroded and disrupted any singular notion of what constitutes a college education.[4] While the depth and breadth of this disruption is debatable, the platforms for such disruption (e.g., MOOCs, digital badges, and competency-based education) and their

undergirding digital learning technologies (e.g., "stealth assessments," adaptive learning, and data analytics) will only become more pervasive.[5]

Don't get me wrong. Colleges and universities as physical places will not disappear. Postsecondary education serves a multiplicity of functions to a wide variety of constituencies. Above and beyond their role in knowledge production and dissemination, postsecondary institutions act as mechanisms of stratification, modes of socialization, drivers of economic activity, and hubs for institutional collaboration.[6] Many of these functions are intertwined with physical communities, and, as such, a large number of place-based colleges and universities will continue to make substantial impacts in their local communities and attract students from around their regions, if not the nation, to their campuses to be taught by faculty, who are at the heart of the academic enterprise.

In addition, technologically driven developments are still often at the beta phase of experimentation, where they function more as supplements to rather than replacements of traditional models of teaching and learning. Moreover, due to a variety of vertical and horizontal patterns of stratification and segmentation, technological disruption will undoubtedly be embraced and embedded differentially across diverse segments of the postsecondary landscape (e.g., nonprofit, for-profit, public, and private two- and four-year institutions).[7] For example, the Massachusetts Institute of Technology and Bunker Hill Community College, although only a few miles apart, will have vastly different implementation strategies and goals for embracing online learning.

At the heart of the problem is the outdated notion that education is solely or simply the delivery of specific content knowledge, transferred from instructors to students

Yet despite their differences, all institutions are affected by the two interrelated points that form the foundation of my provocation: first, that most traditional modes of teaching and learning do a pretty poor job of educating a large percentage of postsecondary students; and second, that technological platforms are increasingly demonstrating their capacity to equal or exceed traditional face-to-face instruction in achieving student outcomes.

A litany of statistics and research suggests that a substantial majority of students are being poorly served by our system of higher education. The evidence includes abysmal graduation rates outside of elite institutions; opportunity and outcome gaps among student populations of different races, ethnicities, and socioeconomic statuses; low-level curriculum delivered in the most important introductory classes; and the deep overreliance on contingent instructors with minimal incentive or support to advance students' success.[8] At the heart of the problem—at least as it concerns civic teaching and learning—is the outdated notion that education is solely or simply the delivery of specific content knowledge, transferred from instructors to students. Such a transmission model of education is flawed, but it was all we had or could hope for beyond the artisanal endeavors of individual faculty.

To date, MOOCs—with their capacity to enroll millions of students anywhere, anytime—have been the most obvious manifestation of the forthcoming technologically driven disruption. These online, massively networked, data-driven, and automated systems are efficient platforms for delivering content, and they are fundamentally changing how we will think of instruction in the future. A plethora of digital learning technologies offer new means of delivering a wide range of content, from "adaptive" modules that change the level of instructional difficulty according to students' responses to automated "stealth assessments" that provide instantaneous feedback and helpful prompts to students based on "big data" mined through sophisticated algorithms.[9]

Such practices are grounded in learning theory that presages the value of such pedagogical practices.[10] It is thus not surprising that recent research has made clear that such online and computer-driven instruction is just as effective as instruction in traditional face-to-face settings. From a 2010 US Department of Education meta-analysis to more recent follow-up studies, research suggests that no particular form of instruction—face-to-face, hybrid, or fully online—is any longer the default mode by which any particular student learns best.[11]

Again, to be clear, I am not suggesting that, broadly speaking, the quintessential seminar—with its intimate small group dynamic driven by a guiding professor and inquisitive students—is somehow in jeopardy of being replaced by a MOOC. But just one in four college students today have followed the traditional path from high school directly into a four-year undergraduate degree program. According to federal data, community colleges educate close to half of the eighteen million students enrolled in postsecondary education.[12] Additionally, a small percent of all college students will ever experience an upper-level seminar like the idyllic one I just described.[13]

In that light, technological solutions become, almost by necessity, an obvious and necessary option for providing adequate instruction to a large number of students at minimal cost. We cannot hide from these realities. That idyllic seminar was never the historical norm and never will be. Instead, we must begin to ask ourselves some important and difficult questions on the future of civic learning that begin in our current reality rather than in some far-away and long-ago seminar dream. Namely, does online education undermine the entire edifice of community-based models of teaching and learning? How does civic learning as a deeply labor-intensive practice continue to resonate in a computer-driven pedagogical environment? What happens to service learning as a critical, justice-oriented, and disruptive pedagogical practice? Put simply, what do we have to offer as civic practitioners?

Civic Learning in an Online World

In fact, I want to suggest that civic learning has much to offer. The distinction—vital to the ultimate value proposition of higher education—is that while MOOCs and other modes of technological disruption may foster better means of instructing and informing, they will never be able to truly educate. They may offer an apprenticeship into Wikipedia, but not an apprenticeship into democracy.

Here, I am referencing the distinction between closed- and open-ended learning, or what learning theorists have alternatively described as shallow and deep learning, first- and second-loop learning, or the difference between the transmission and transformation models of education.[14] This distinction—which, yes, may be too binary and neat—nevertheless offers a productive way of understanding the limits of technological disruption and its potential for inspiring a renewed vision for civic learning.

The distinction is that computer-based technologies are incredibly efficient at processing well-defined tasks within closed-loop systems. They can transmit specific content in multiple ways, assess students' comprehension in real time, provide immediate feedback, and offer highly calibrated next steps that adapt to an individual's particular background knowledge, level of comprehension, and learning preferences. This is learning analytics at its best, and we will begin to see much more of such technological sophistication in the coming years embedded within online modules and learning platforms.[15]

But such an instructional model has prescribed limits. Specifically, the content knowledge it delivers must involve right and wrong answers.[16] When a lesson can be taught by atomizing a body of knowledge and delimiting the parameters of acceptable responses, an automated system will excel. This is coming to be known as the "modularization" of the curriculum, as information is chunked into more precise nuggets of information able to be taught in specific and tightly orchestrated increments.[17]

Yet such a mode of instruction never can (nor was meant to) replace the transformational role of education.[18] The educational moment of grappling with the complexities and ambiguities of any difficult and non-binary problem cannot be captured in such modularization of the curriculum. This is because any educational attempt to step outside of a preconfigured and prepared system, to, for example, jump a level of awareness in order to survey the system's context, assumptions, and implications, reveals the system's "brittleness"—its inability to handle ambiguous or unexpected developments.[19]

Such moments of uncertainty, which force us to rethink and reorient our notions of what is normal, are crucial. John Dewey, in *How We Think*, poetically described such "moments of doubt" as presenting a "forked-road situation" that fosters true thinking, "a situation which is ambiguous, which presents a dilemma, which proposes alternatives" that force us to pause and "metaphorically climb a tree; we try to find some standpoint from which we may survey additional facts and, getting a more commanding view of the situation, may decide how the facts stand related to one another."[20] These moments ultimately represent the notion of education as transformation rather than as transmission. They allow us to step outside of ourselves and, in fact, see ourselves.

The possibility of moments like these is the power and promise of civic learning in higher education—not as a supplement to the traditional transmission model of education, but as the fundamental model of education in the disrupted university. For if students can gain college credit through learning modules and online courses, then all that is left, all we have to hold onto, all that makes true education worthwhile, lies within the sphere of civic learning.

What civic learning thus offers is exactly those "moments of doubt" that cannot be fully prescribed or anticipated: moments of stepping outside of the normal, engaging in "boundary crossing," and fostering and forcing reflection. Whether referred to as service learning, community-based research, or civic engagement, such practices are inherently complex. By their very nature, they require engaging with the complicated realities of our day-to-day lives and they disrupt our taken-for-granted notions of the world.[21] The disrupted university may thus actually allow us to begin to put the disruptive potential of civic learning at the center rather than the periphery of our educational practices.

I do not mean this, though, in the rhetorical way employed by some civic learning advocates.[22] I think of it in very pragmatic terms. Technological disruption will allow students to engage in learning in their own ways and at their own paces. Students already learn particular content knowledge through a wide variety of online courses, web-based modules (such as Khan Academy videos and TED talks), and MOOC-type learning management platforms. By unbundling instructional practices from seat time spent at place-based institutions, the disrupted university undermines any notion of a center. Students can learn and demonstrate mastery of their learning anywhere, anytime, in any way.

What civic learning thus offers, through place-based institutions and faculty-guided instruction, is the opportunity to integrate and extend such knowledge into the real world. Think of this as the flipped classroom expanded to the entire university. In the "flipped university," students enact and operationalize their knowledge, which is integrated with meaningful engagement in mutually reinforcing ways. The flipped university offers a visible manifestation of civic learning as it links theory and practice in the public sphere by having students actually engage with the learning that they have already done through other platforms.

The disrupted university may thus actually allow us to begin to put the disruptive potential of civic learning at the center rather than the periphery of our educational practices

This, of course, already occurs in multiple ways across higher education, from project-based learning to labs, from internships to service learning. But in the flipped university, such civic practices, rather than being the purview of a select few students and faculty, could become the norm and the embodiment of an educated person. They could become what college credit signifies.

My provocation is that the forthcoming technological disruption is a good thing because it will force us to confront and enact what engaged learning in the public sphere could actually be. It will force us, for example, to begin granting academic credit not for being instructed, but for putting instruction into practice; to require that students demonstrate that learning matters to who they want to become; to prioritize impact over seat time; and to accept that assessing civic learning is a shared enterprise that transcends any single standardized measure. Put otherwise, if civic learning is indeed about linking theory and practice to foster critical inquiry and democratic engagement, then our educational models must begin to scaffold, support, assess, and reward students' civic engagement at every level of the system.

CONCLUDING THOUGHTS

The transition I have described above is profound, and it will be difficult to enact. It will require a rethinking of what it means to teach and learn on a college campus and of the pedagogical and organizational infrastructures that support teaching and learning. It will mean placing components that used to be considered add-ons, such as service learning, internships, and alternative capstone projects, at the heart and soul of the learning experience.

What such a re-centering would portend, if we could accomplish it, is a "civic learning 2.0" that is revitalized rather than ravaged by the forthcoming technological disruption. In fact, the forthcoming disruption will be an opportunity to align the power of technology with the longstanding vision of higher education.

In conclusion, I want to note that there is really nothing radical in this idea that a college education should help students learn how to engage with real-world problems and issues, develop competence in areas ranging from quantitative reasoning to critical inquiry to communication, and gain the habits of mind and repertoires of action necessary to demonstrate such capacities thoughtfully and meaningfully. We have wanted this for generations.

What is radical is the idea that such an education might actually be possible now. But enacting it will require an articulation of next steps that is dramatically different from how we have thought of teaching and learning until now. We cannot conduct business as usual. It is thus incumbent on those of us who work and teach in higher education to make clear to ourselves and to the larger public that education is about deep learning—and that such civic learning cannot be found solely in the online cloud. It requires us and our students to have our feet on the ground.

NOTES

1. The "disruption" of higher education is a highly contested notion. See Dan Butin, "From MOOCs to Dragons," *Inside Higher Ed*, April 14, 2014, http://www.insidehighered.com/blogs/higher-ed-beta/moocs-dragons, for my analysis of how such technologically-driven change is impacting higher education. I take "civic learning" as a broad indicator of the interconnected pedagogical practices and philosophical stances (e.g., service learning, participatory action research, community-based research) that experientially engage students through academic coursework in their local and global communities. Civic learning may be broadly defined as the knowledge, skills, values, and collective actions that "emphasize the civic significance of preparing students with knowledge and for action…. [in] a highly diverse and globally engaged democracy." The National Task Force on Civic Learning and Democratic Engagement, *A Crucible Moment: College Learning and Democracy's Future* (Washington, DC: Association of American Colleges and Universities, 2012), 3. However, it is important to note, as Finley and many others have suggested, that "civic engagement is a term that lacks a cohesive definition." Ashley Finley, "Civic Learning and Democratic Engagements: A Review of the Literature on Civic Engagement in Post-Secondary Education" (paper prepared for the United States Department of Education, Association of American Colleges and Universities, Washington, DC, May 24, 2011), 20. See also Dan W. Butin, *Service-Learning in Theory and Practice: The Future of Community Engagement in Higher Education* (New York: Palgrave Macmillan, 2010).

2. See, for example, William G. Bowen, *Higher Education in the Digital Age* (Princeton, NJ: Princeton University Press, 2013), regarding how such a "digital" future may look and Candace Thille, *Changing the Production Function in Higher Education* (Washington DC: American Council on Education, 2012) for the undergirding relevance—pedagogical and budgetary—of digital technologies.

3. For an expansion on these ideas, see Dan W. Butin, "There's No App for Ending Racism: Theorizing the Civic in an Age of Disruption," *Diversity & Democracy* 17, no. 1 (2014): 11–13.

4. See James G. Mazoué, "The Deconstructed Campus," *Journal of Computing in Higher Education* 24, no. 2 (2012): 74–95.

5. See Thomas Carey and David Trick, *How Online Learning Affects Productivity, Cost and Quality in*

Higher Education: An Environmental Scan and Review of the Literature (Toronto: Higher Education Quality Council of Ontario, 2013); and Patricia W. Neely and Jan P. Tucker, "Unbundling Faculty Roles in Online Distance Education Programs," *International Review of Research in Open and Distance Learning* 11, no. 2 (2010): http://www.irrodl.org/index.php/irrodl/article/view/798/1543.

6. See Mitchell L. Stevens, Elizabeth A. Armstrong, and Richard Arum, "Sieve, Incubator, Temple, Hub: Empirical and Theoretical Advances in the Sociology of Higher Education," *Annual Review in Sociology* 34 (2008): 127–51.

7. Scott Davies and David Zarifa, "The Stratification of Universities: Structural Inequality in Canada and the United States," *Research in Social Stratification and Mobility* 30, no. 2 (2012): 143–58.

8. See, for example, Richard Arum and Josipa Roksa, *Academically Adrift: Limited Learning on College Campuses* (Chicago: University of Chicago Press, 2011) regarding students' academic success and Ann L. Mullen, *Degrees of Inequality: Culture, Class, and Gender in American Higher Education* (Baltimore: Johns Hopkins University Press, 2010) regarding how such success is stratified across different student groups. See Sara E. Brownell and Kimberly D. Tanner, "Barriers to Faculty Pedagogical Change: Lack of Training, Time, Incentives, and Tensions with Professional Identity?" *CBE–Life Sciences Education* 11, no. 4 (2012): 339–46 and Diane Ebert-May, Terry L. Derting, Janet Hodder, Jennifer L. Momsen, Tammy M. Long, and Sarah E. Jardeleza, "What We Say Is Not What We Do: Effective Evaluation of Faculty Professional Development Programs," *BioScience* 61, no. 7 (2011): 550–58 regarding the difficulty of supporting faculty in high-quality instruction.

9. See Adam Cooper, "What is Analytics? Definition and Essential Characteristics," *CETIS Analytics Series* 1, no. 5 (2012).

10. David George Glance, Martin Forsey, and Myles Riley, "The Pedagogical Foundations of Massive Open Online Courses," *First Monday* 18, no. 5 (2013), http://firstmonday.org/ojs/index.php/fm/article/view/4350/3673.

11. See William G. Bowen, Matthew M. Chingos, Kelly A. Lack, and Thomas I. Nygren, "Interactive Learning Online at Public Universities: Evidence from a Six Campus Randomized Trial," *Journal of Policy Analysis and Management* 33, no. 1 (2013): 94–111; Kelly A. Lack, *Current Status of Research on Online Learning in Postsecondary Education* (New York: Ithaka S+R, 2013), http://www.sr.ithaka.org/sites/default/files/reports/ithaka-sr-online-learning-postsecondary-education-may2012.pdf; and Barbara Means, Yukie Toyama, Robert Murphy, Marianne Bakia, and Karla Jones, *Evaluation of Evidence-Based Practices in Online Learning: A Meta-Analysis and Review of Online Learning Studies* (Washington, DC: US Department of Education, 2010), http://www2.ed.gov/rschstat/eval/tech/evidence-based-practices/finalreport.pdf.

12. See Susan Aud, Sidney Wilkinson-Flicker, Paul Kristapovich, Amy Rathbun, Xiaolei Wang, and Jijun Zhang, *The Condition of Education 2013* (Washington, DC: US Department of Education, National Center for Education Statistics, 2013).

13. See George D. Kuh and Ken O'Donnell, *Ensuring Quality and Taking High-Impact Practices to Scale* (Washington, DC: Association of American Colleges and Universities, 2013).

14. See, for example, Gregory Bateson, *Steps to an Ecology of Mind: Collected Essays in Anthropology, Psychiatry, Evolution, and Epistemology* (Chicago: University of Chicago Press, 2000); Jack Mezirow, "Transformative Learning: Theory to Practice," *New Directions for Adult and Continuing Education* 1997, no. 74 (1997): 5–12; and Donald A. Schön, *The Reflective Practitioner: How Professionals Think in Action* (New York: Basic Books, 1983).

15. See President's Council of Advisors on Science and Technology (PCAST), letter to the President of the United States, December 2013, http://www.whitehouse.gov/sites/default/files/microsites/ostp/PCAST/pcast_edit_dec-2013.pdf.

16. See Kurt VanLehn, "The Relative Effectiveness of Human Tutoring, Intelligent Tutoring Systems, and Other Tutoring Systems," *Educational Psychologist* 46, no. 4 (2011): 197–221.

17. Institute-wide Task Force on the Future of MIT Education, *Preliminary Report* (Cambridge, MA: Massachusetts Institute of Technology, 2013), http://web.mit.edu/future-report/TaskForceOnFutureOfMITEducation_PrelimReport.pdf.

18. See Sanjay Sarma and Isaac Chuang, "The Magic Beyond the MOOCs," *MIT Faculty Newsletter* 25, no. 5 (2013), http://web.mit.edu/fnl/volume/255/sarmay_chuang.html.

19. For the basis of this insight, see Bateson, *Steps to an Ecology of Mind*; for an expansion as it relates to civic learning, see chapter 3 of Butin, *Service-Learning in Theory and Practice*.

20. John Dewey, *How We Think* (New York: Heath & Co., 1910), 11.

21. See Tania D. Mitchell, "Traditional vs. Critical Service-Learning: Engaging the Literature to Differentiate Two Models," *Michigan Journal of Community Service Learning* 14, no. 2 (2008): 50–65.

22. See, for example, National Task Force on Civic Learning, *A Crucible Moment*.

(Social) Justice for All (Undergraduate Degree Programs): Institutionalizing Critical Civic Literacy in the Undergraduate Curriculum

2

Seth Pollack

… and to the Republic, for which it stands, one Nation under God, indivisible, with liberty and justice for all.—PLEDGE OF ALLEGIANCE

WE HAVE ALL HEARD THESE WORDS MANY TIMES. But what does "justice for all" actually mean in the context of our daily lives as higher education professionals, members of local communities, citizens of this nation, and even global citizens? As a professor of service learning at California State University–Monterey Bay (CSUMB), I have thought repeatedly about this phrase over the past two decades while working with colleagues at CSUMB to integrate critical civic literacy, with its focus on social justice, into the core of the university's required service-learning program.[1] This integration has meant joining forces with degree programs across campus to create curricula that help students examine the interfaces between the personal and the public, the corporate and the commons, their individual careers and the quality of life in their communities. Through critical civic literacy, students develop deeper relationships to issues of social justice and equity in the context of their personal lives and their future professions.

As I have shared CSUMB's work on critical civic literacy at national conferences and other academic gatherings, I have noticed a significant disconnect between our nation's collective, passive understanding of the words "and justice for all" as recited in the Pledge of Allegiance, and how we as higher education professionals have come to understand the place of social justice in the core curriculum. Speaking in various venues over the last twenty years, I have seen looks of profound disbelief or astonishment on the faces of colleagues from other institutions as I describe the organizing frameworks and principles of CSUMB's service-learning program. As I have discussed CSUMB's service-learning requirement and the core learning outcomes related to service, social justice, and multicultural community building that the institution has integrated into every undergraduate major, I have seen colleagues listening with strained looks on their faces, struggling to make sense of the CSUMB story in the context of their own institutional realities. Nodding politely, but with brows fully furrowed, they are often thinking to themselves, "Your faculty and students must be entirely different from the faculty and students at my institution." They often comment,

"Your students must not be juggling their studies with full-time work responsibilities and responsibilities at home, like our students are. Our students would never have time for this." And when reflecting on the popular recent trend of questioning the high cost of higher education and its ultimate value in the job market, they often say, "CSUMB must somehow be insulated from the broader societal and political forces that are emphasizing workforce preparation as the fundamental purpose of a college degree." They ask, "How could we at CSUMB devote such significant curricular space to the WEP (Well-Educated Person) when the discourse in higher education is focused on ROI (Return on Investment)?"

Higher education has embraced service learning as an effective form of engaged and engaging pedagogy, but not as a legitimate area of knowledge or content

Why is it so easy to say a pledge that emphasizes the value of "liberty and justice for all," but so difficult to imagine a higher education institution where all degree programs require students to think deeply about issues of liberty and justice and to become involved, through service learning, in addressing the injustices that exist in our neighborhoods, communities, and nation, as well as across the globe? Why, despite decades of faculty effort, do civic engagement programs in higher education still fail to address questions of equity and justice with the necessary depth, and why do they remain located tenuously on the margins of higher education?

In order for critical civic literacy to be a central component of undergraduate education, we need to create space at the core of our degree programs for legitimate discussion of issues of justice and equity. Unfortunately, the governing institutional forces have not made it easy for higher education to embrace critical civic literacy at the core of its mission. Paradigms are not easy to change, as they are the products of decades-old normative and cognitive structures and rule systems that determine what belongs and how things should be. For concepts like civic literacy that have been struggling in the margins to become more central in higher education, it will take a critical mass of people and programs to rework norms and rewrite definitions.

WHY IS EMBRACING CRITICAL CIVIC LITERACY
SO HARD FOR HIGHER EDUCATION?

A closer look at the dominant paradigm behind the response to CSUMB's critical civic literacy efforts suggests some of the forces that keep these efforts marginalized across higher education. An examination of these forces sheds light on the taken-for-granted norms, expectations, and patterns of interaction that keep social justice–oriented civic engagement efforts on the fringe while reinforcing the hegemony of higher education's expert-oriented, discipline-based approach to knowledge production and transmission. I briefly summarize four of these forces below.

1. *Higher education has embraced service learning as an effective form of engaged and engaging pedagogy, but not as a legitimate area of knowledge or content.* While administrative units supporting faculty in implementing service-learning projects have proliferated across higher education, service-learning requirements have not

been similarly adopted by universities or departments. Why not? It's simple. The disciplines have largely embraced service learning as a teaching technique or pedagogy, but not as an area of study or content. Academic departments do not require instructors to employ specific teaching techniques in their courses; through academic requirements, departments define what knowledge is to be learned, not how that knowledge is to be taught. While 96 percent of Campus Compact members report having a campus center devoted to community and civic engagement,[2] CSUMB is one of only a handful of higher education institutions that have implemented a service-learning requirement for all undergraduate programs. Where service learning has spread in higher education, its proliferation has largely been a result of faculty embracing it as an effective strategy to teach traditional disciplinary knowledge, not as a way to examine complex issues related to service and social justice, equity and diversity, identity and belonging, the public and the private. While some room for examining students' civic learning has existed on the margins of higher education, academic programs have largely emphasized using the service experience to help students apply and master traditional disciplinary knowledge and become better readers, writers, and arithmeticians through active, engaged learning in the community. Higher education has embraced service learning, but as a teaching tool, not as a content area.

2. *Departments traditionally have the ultimate authority over the curriculum and are resistant to embracing externally generated and collectively shared outcomes that cross disciplines, such as critical civic literacy.* There is an organizational impediment to the integration of critical civic literacy within academic departments and programs, grounded in the fact that departments have authority over and control of the knowledge base. The idea of embracing content generated by an outside entity, such as a university office of civic engagement, or the community for that matter, runs contrary to the idea that disciplines and departments are the guardians of their knowledge base, responsible for determining curricular content. Although they have reluctantly embraced areas of content that their professional associations define as relevant, departments have traditionally resisted yielding authority over the content of their curricula to those outside their disciplines or professional fields. As a result, where it occurs at all, the conversation about civic engagement exists on the fringes of the university, far from the centers of curricular content and influence.

3. *Departments and degree programs have varying levels of comfort with the social justice–oriented issues that are at the heart of critical civic literacy, and with the overall goal of helping students become "multicultural community-builders."*[3] Critical civic literacy requires engaging with issues of justice and equity and examining one's own relationship to various dimensions of social inequity. While faculty in some departments and degree programs (i.e., those in sociology, ethnic studies, or other areas of the humanities) would find these learning outcomes familiar and allied to the core content of their fields, faculty in other departments (i.e., those in the sciences or professional fields, such as information technology) might have more trouble seeing their disciplines and fields as directly contributing to the goal of educating multicultural community-builders. This is

especially apparent in the current climate, where departments are under pressure to reduce time to degree while embracing their fields' rapidly expanding technical knowledge bases and preparing students to graduate with the skills needed by the workforce. With these pressures, it is difficult for issues of social responsibility, social justice, and civic identity and engagement—all of which are at the heart of critical civic literacy—to find curricular space.

4. *Even if critical civic literacy is a legitimate goal for all degree programs, faculty members in most departments do not have the backgrounds or expertise to facilitate learning about issues of social justice or systemic inequality.* In the dominant paradigm, faculty might argue, "We are scientists, not ethicists"; "We are business faculty, and our focus is on profit and efficiency, not justice and equity." Furthermore, issues of social justice and systemic inequality are full of moral dilemmas— which the dominant paradigm places outside of the scope of the university, whose foundation is built on uncovering objective truths. In the dominant paradigm, faculty ask, "Shouldn't such discussions more appropriately take place in the home, or at church, synagogue, mosque, or temple?"

Taken together, these four factors represent the dominant paradigm in higher education's reaction to service learning and other efforts at transformative civic engagement work. While service learning has both a pedagogical dimension (the "how to" of engaged experiential learning) and an epistemological dimension (the "content" related to issues of service, diversity, democracy, and social justice), the dominant forces in higher education have served to marginalize the epistemological dimension, while enthusiastically embracing service-learning and other forms of civic engagement as pedagogical tools. I have called this process *pedagogification*: the reworking of an epistemologically transformative educational practice into a teaching method, stripping the initiative of its potentially transformative content while emphasizing its utility as a tool for mastering the traditional knowledge base.[4]

Through the process of pedagogification, higher education has been able to embrace service learning and other civic engagement efforts while still maintaining the norms, definitions, and structures that control what is legitimate knowledge (i.e., the curriculum); who are legitimate holders of knowledge (i.e., professors); and who determines the content of the curriculum (i.e., the academic departments). As a result, while scholars have documented a tremendous increase in civic action by students and the emergence of a plethora of policy statements supporting civic engagement by higher education leaders over the past three decades, structures have not emerged, either at colleges and universities or within academic departments, to support sustained, systemic civic literacy efforts.[5] In a particularly insightful comment, John Saltmarsh and Matthew Hartley summarize their striking conclusion that while the goal of engagement has been to transform higher education by reviving its civic mission, engagement itself has been transformed:

All too often, service learning courses are indistinguishable from internships or clinical placements: their chief aim is disciplinary learning or improved clinical practice. Democratic outcomes—encouraging students to understand and question the social and political factors that cause social problems and to challenge and change them—at best remain hoped-for by-products.[6]

WHAT IT TAKES TO INSTITUTIONALIZE CRITICAL CIVIC LITERACY

Paradigms are powerful, as they inform how we, and the institutions that we are a part of, are expected to act. But they are not otherworldly in their creation. In fact, they are constructed and reconstructed by the daily actions and interactions of individuals as they participate in organizational life. Constructing a different paradigm means consciously acting to create and institutionalize new definitions, norms, and expectations for both individuals and the institutions that they embody. CSUMB's contra-paradigmatic work provides insights that might help higher education move beyond the pedagogification of service learning to more fully embrace the transformational potential of critical civic literacy. What can be learned from CSUMB's successful effort to construct and maintain a model of service learning in which there is "[social] justice for all [undergraduate degree programs]"? And how has CSUMB developed this capacity in all departments across the campus? The following are some of the crucial factors that have served to support CSUMB's rich embrace of critical civic literacy.

Both the pedagogical and epistemological dimensions of critical civic literacy must be institutionally supported. While most service-learning and civic engagement units on campuses exist to support other academic programs or are housed on the student affairs side, strong connections with the academic side of the university are necessary for these units to effectively address both the pedagogical and epistemological dimensions of civic literacy. At their core, civic-literacy efforts must be seen by academic departments as representing legitimate and essential areas of knowledge that are critical for student learning and success.

Both the pedagogical and epistemological dimensions of critical civic literacy must be institutionally supported

Organizationally, the Service Learning Institute (SLI) at CSUMB embodies both the pedagogical and epistemological aspects of service learning. It serves as both an academic support unit, providing training and support for service-learning pedagogy campus-wide, and as a formal academic department, responsible for curriculum development and delivery of instruction. The SLI staff includes tenured and tenure-track professors of service learning who design and teach courses and offer a minor in service learning leadership, along with a variety of support staff who provide logistical and partnership support for all service-learning courses campus-wide.

CSUMB's curriculum development framework, the Service Learning Prism, (*see page 14*), also embodies a bridge between the pedagogical/epistemological duality.[7] The Service Learning Prism blurs the boundaries between pedagogy and content, calling faculty to recognize that knowledge outside of the textbook is critical for student learning. The pedagogical dimension of service learning is represented by the three sources of knowledge (or beams of light) that enter the prism: discipline-based knowledge, student knowledge, and community knowledge. Recognizing these three distinct and legitimate sources of knowledge requires faculty to move from a framework where the discipline is the sole source of knowledge to a student-centered and ultimately an experiential learning framework where the student and the community are also seen as legitimate sources of knowledge that are essential to the learning process. Faculty must master moving from the "sage on the stage," where they are seen as the sole source of legitimate knowledge, to the "guide on the side" in order to facilitate students' integration of disciplinary knowledge with their own prior knowledge and with the community knowledge they experience through their service work.

CSUMB Service Learning Prism

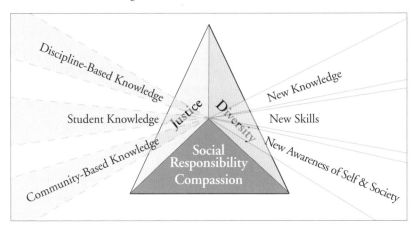

The epistemological or content dimension of service learning is represented by the concepts within the prism itself: justice, compassion, diversity, and social responsibility. These four concepts are at the heart of CSUMB's understanding of critical civic literacy. With these concepts at the center, the prism emphasizes that issues of service and social justice are not marginal afterthoughts, but rather are fundamental to transforming the learning that occurs through a service-learning course. In a service-learning course guided by the prism's framework, the student does not merely do service in the community in order to master the knowledge and skills of the discipline or field. Rather, the student comes away from the course with new knowledge, new skills, and a new awareness of herself and her relationship to issues of justice and equity in the world around her. Thus the prism represents one approach to civic literacy where content about service, social responsibility, and justice is fully present at the core of the academic endeavor.

Academic culture must value outcomes-based education and take seriously university-wide goals for student learning and the university's relationship to its surrounding communities. By adopting an outcomes-based educational approach to student learning, faculty become prepared to embrace the idea that there are constructs (learning outcomes) that they are accountable for addressing in their courses in both general education and in the majors. A focus on interdisciplinary and project-based learning also helps the faculty embrace an approach to education that uses real-world problems and social realities as contexts for student learning. These factors soften the walls that separate the disciplines and to some extent facilitate the department's willingness to engage with content areas that faculty traditionally see as outside of their particular realms of expertise.

CSUMB's system of university-wide learning outcomes has provided an important mechanism to transform the vague statements and broad concepts embodied in the university's vision statement into concrete student learning objectives, including critical civic literacy. It has also created a system of accountability and a of concepts around which faculty come together across disciplines for extensive professional development work.[8] As a comprehensive university that embraces the institutional value of regional stewardship, CSUMB has placed the issues confronting the region's communities at the center of its curriculum and made them the focus of faculty and student engagement. CSUMB reinforces this centrality with a unique retention, tenure, and promotion policy that includes "professional application" as a critical fourth area of scholarship in addition to the traditional areas of teaching, research, and university service.[9] As a result, all CSUMB faculty are expected to apply their professional knowledge and skills in collaboration with the external community to address critical community issues while strengthening CSUMB's role as a steward of place.

Course learning outcomes must be grounded in issues of equity and justice that are relevant to the discipline and to the local, regional, or global community. The separation between an individual's professional life and his civic life should be blurred. Degree programs should explore the intersection between particular technical or theoretical fields of study and the social inequities that exist in our communities.

At CSUMB, the service-learning curriculum development process begins at this point, with faculty identifying social justice issues that are pertinent to their field of study and to communities in the region. These issues become the guiding social justice meta-questions that inform the entire curriculum development process and are the basis for specific service-learning outcomes that faculty identify for their courses. In the traditional paradigm, the service-learning curriculum development process usually starts with the question, "What can my students *do* in the community that allows them to use the knowledge they acquire in the course?" In contrast, the critical civic literacy approach starts with the question, "What is the *overarching question* about equity and social justice that I want my students to critically examine through this course?" By responding to this question, preferably through collaborative discussions with community partners, faculty can develop learning outcomes and identify service opportunities that are relevant for the field or discipline, that matter to the community, and that are deeply grounded in issues of justice and equity.

Institutions must commit to building capacity for critical civic literacy by offering training opportunities, recruiting relevant expertise, and embracing the powerful role of students as peer educators. Facilitating student learning about issues of diversity, identity, social justice, and systemic inequality is challenging. Topics like racism, sexism, classism, homophobia, and other forms of oppression have very personal dimensions, and classroom discussions of these issues often become highly charged. Higher education leadership needs to acknowledge that while our faculties are full of brilliant individuals who have been trained as experts in wide variety of fields, very few faculty members have been trained to be experts in facilitating learning about social justice and systemic inequality. And yet, that expertise is essentially what we are asking of faculty when we ask them to teach critical civic literacy.

With a task like memorizing the periodic table in chemistry, each individual participating in the exercise has a similar, objective relationship to the content. In contrast, learning about issues of social power, systemic inequality, privilege, and oppression is highly individual and personal. Each person has a complex web of identities and positionalities that result in different relationships to the knowledge base itself. Furthermore, these positionalities likely corresponded to very different life experiences and interactions, with each individual inhabiting a very different world and developing very different worldviews or truths. Therefore, teaching about issues of oppression and privilege requires faculty to facilitate simultaneously the many diverse journeys that are taking place in the classroom. To master the subject matter of critical civic literacy, each student must follow a different learning trajectory, requiring different learning and unlearning depending on his or her social identities, positionalities, and life experiences. Facilitating this type of learning requires a very different skill set from teaching more static content like the periodic table.

As faculty leadership in CSUMB's academic departments have come to own the critical civic literacy dimension of the core curriculum, they have begun to recognize the critical importance of having faculty members with this relevant expertise. As a result, the departments have begun to search for and hire tenure-track faculty with backgrounds in service learning and research interests and experience related to social justice education. Additionally, CSUMB's Service Learning Institute offers professional development activities to strengthen faculty members' knowledge and skills related to critical civic literacy by:

- providing faculty with a wealth of readings, classroom activities, and other resources to help them address service-learning outcomes, and offering training programs to facilitate the adoption and integration of these outcomes into diverse curricula;
- sharing techniques on how to build trust in the classroom and create a compassionate and courageous space where students can share and explore their experiences with issues of inequality;
- working with faculty to help them examine how issues of privilege and oppression have affected their own lives and career paths—a reflective process that is an essential prerequisite to teaching critical civic literacy;
- helping faculty use personal narratives, especially their own, to model the power and validity of personal experience as a valuable source of knowledge.

Finally, by serving as peer educators, CSUMB students have played an important role in supporting faculty in the challenging task of teaching about power, privilege, and social inequality. As peers, trained student leaders can provide a powerful starting point for students to talk authentically about their own experiences with issues of power, privilege, and oppression. Working as co-educators with faculty, student leaders can reinforce the validity of their peers' life experiences as valuable sources of knowledge. These leaders can also blur traditional boundaries around who has knowledge and how knowledge is acquired, strengthening students' sense of efficacy and their capacity for meaningful engagement. Supported by peer educators, students begin to experience a powerful process of meaning-making. They begin to build on their own life experiences to plot new ways of acting that undermine the systems of oppression and privilege that continue to separate people and limit opportunities for diverse community members.

CONCLUSION: CONSTRUCTING A NEW PARADIGM

Challenging the dominant paradigm of civic learning in higher education means moving from a pedagogified approach focused on service learning and civic engagement to an approach that embraces critical civic literacy. Such a move has concrete implications for service learning and other civic engagement programs. First, it means seeing service learning as more than a pedagogy; it is an approach with content and a knowledge base that need to be presented explicitly in courses and degree programs. Second, it means making more permeable the narrow authority structures that control what is understood to be legitimate knowledge in departments and degree programs, so that these departments and programs can more effectively address the broad, interdisciplinary realities related to service, social justice, and inequality that exist in our communities. Third, it means explicitly articulating and teaching to issues of equity and justice as areas of core content within degree programs. Departments need to make explicit the relationship between their academic fields and the inequality that exists in our communities. Understanding the forces that contribute to inequality and alienation in our communities, our nation, and around the world should not be a task solely for faculty and students in sociology and philosophy programs. All graduates need the skills to build such understanding if higher education hopes to subvert the global trends toward increasing economic inequality and sectarian factionalism (whether ethnic, religious, or of another nature) that are fraying the tapestry of societal civility.

Finally, higher education needs to develop the expertise across its departments and disciplines to facilitate learning about critical civic literacy, allowing students to bring the realities of their own diverse positionalities and life experiences into the classroom in a way that brings meaning to their lives and activates their potential as change agents. Student peer educators are a powerful, and largely untapped, resource to help educators do the transformational teaching and learning that students deserve, and that our globalized, highly stratified, and increasingly unequal world requires. If higher education is to contribute to building the more fully inclusive society that today's world demands, then "(social) justice for all (undergraduate programs)" must become a reality.

NOTES

1. All students at CSUMB complete two service-learning courses as part of their graduation requirements, both of which teach to what we call "critical civic literacy." Students take a general education course in the lower division that introduces them to concepts of service, diversity, identity, social justice, and community building. They then take a second course in their major, where they revisit these "critical civic literacy" themes—but this time, from the perspective of their major field of study. "Critical civic literacy" emphasizes the effect of power relations and social group identities on opportunities and participation in public life, and stresses the examination

of root causes of systemic social problems. "Critical civic literacy" seeks to develop in students the knowledge, skills and attitudes needed to become aware of and bring about change in these oppressive social structures as an essential component of civic learning.

2. Campus Compact, *2012 Annual Member Survey: Creating a Culture of Assessment* (Boston: Campus Compact, 2012), 7.

3. The overarching goal of the CSUMB program is to develop multicultural community builders, which CSUMB defines as "students who have the knowledge, skills and attitudes to work effectively in a diverse society and to create more just and equitable workplaces, communities, and social institutions." See California State University–Monterey Bay Service Learning Institute, "What is a *Multicultural Community Builder?*" (handout, California State University–Monterey Bay, 2003), http://service.csumb.edu/sites/default/files/101/igx_migrate/files/SLI0100.pdf.

4. Seth Pollack, "Critical Civic Literacy as a Core Component of Undergraduate Education," in *Community Engagement in Higher Education: Policy Reforms and Practice*, ed. W. James Jacob, Stewart E. Sutin, John C. Weidman, and John L. Yeager (Rotterdam, Netherlands: Sense Publishers, forthcoming).

5. See Kellogg Commission on the Future of State and Land-Grant Universities, *Returning to Our Roots: Executive Summaries of the Reports of the Kellogg Commission on the Future of State and Land-Grant Universities* (New York: Association of Public and Land-Grant Universities, 2001), http://aplu.org/NetCommunity/Document.Doc?id=187; and John Saltmarsh, Matthew Hartley, and Patti Clayton, *Democratic Engagement White Paper* (Boston: New England Resource Center for Higher Education, 2009), http://futureofengagement.files.wordpress.com/2009/02/democratic-engagement-white-paper-2_13_09.pdf.

6. John Saltmarsh and Matthew Hartley, eds., *"To Serve a Larger Purpose": Engagement for Democracy and the Transformation of Higher Education* (Philadelphia: Temple University Press, 2011), 290.

7. For a complete explanation of the Service Learning Prism, see http://service.csumb.edu/sli-overview/sl-prism.

8. The CSUMB campus is currently developing a common set of baccalaureate outcomes guided by Lumina Foundation's Degree Qualifications Profile. These outcomes will provide an even broader set of guiding frameworks to ensure coherence and accountability to a common set of comprehensive goals for student learning. Though the framework is in its preliminary stages, Civic Engagement and Multicultural Community Building is currently one of its major components. For information about the Degree Qualifications Profile, see Lumina Foundation, *The Degree Qualifications Profile* (Washington, DC: Lumina Foundation for Education, Inc., 2011).

9. "Retention, Tenure and Promotion Policy," revised 2011, California State University–Monterey Bay, http://ap.csumb.edu/retention-tenure-promotion.

Strategies for Understanding the Impact of Civic Learning and Teaching

3

Barbara Holland

OVER THE LAST TWENTY-FIVE YEARS, the greatest effort in higher education among civic practitioners regarding civic learning and teaching has been given to building the field and making a case for the objectives and purposes of engagement. In contrast, less attention has been devoted to examining the field with a critical eye, looking to capture the effects of civic learning strategies on students, community, and faculty so as to understand what creates or inhibits those effects. Energy and attention of practitioners and scholars on campuses has mainly focused on the designing of different modalities of civic learning—such as service learning, community-based learning, alternative breaks, days of service, and global learning—and on advocating internally to generate the senior-level strategic and financial support needed to sustain a growing number of civic learning activities. To be frank, this intense advocacy for particular civic learning models sometimes resulted in programs that seemed to exist for their own sake. Worse, the focus on "letting every flower bloom" has often resulted in programs that serve a few lucky students, leaving others with little or no exposure to civic learning. This random approach can result in unequal access and experiences among students and communities as well as episodic interactions between institutions and civic entities, with uncertain outcomes for all involved. Civic learning agendas that lack the organizing logic necessary to intentionally connect institutional expertise, student learning goals, and community interests and goals can result in situations where students and faculty end up "visiting" or "learning about" communities in a superficial or temporary way, without necessarily generating any significant change or impact for either students or the community. Missing from these approaches is a clear and strategic rationale for implementing new civic learning activities—a rationale that would provide institutions with a framework and a clear set of goals for measuring effectiveness and outcomes, for both the students and the community.

Recently, practitioners and scholars have given attention to a more integrated and strategic view of civic learning and engagement strategies, and to the intentional use of monitoring and measurement systems as a means of capturing evidence that may substantiate impacts and suggest ideas for program improvement. This trend toward greater interest in documenting, evaluating, and measuring the impacts of an institution's civic agenda is opening new possibilities for building a deeper understanding of how students, community partners, and faculty learn, explore, and innovate together over time. Such an understanding will significantly advance higher education's performance generally and its civic mission in particular. Additionally, an increasing number of colleges and universities are working with their community partners to develop focused agendas for institution-wide work on a few specific but broadly framed public issues or opportunities, increasing the potential for measurable change and progress for all involved. Built around topics such as sustainability, obesity, and literacy, this issues-based approach is a powerful antidote to random, episodic, and disconnected civic interactions that are not linked sufficiently to specific student learning and developmental outcomes, or that are not substantial enough in time, content, and effort to produce desired effects in community capacity.

Documenting, evaluating, and measuring an institution's civic agenda opens possibilities for deepening understanding of how students, community partners, and faculty learn, explore, and innovate together over time

These signs of greater intentionality toward civic engagement agendas are timely, having emerged just as the conditions that underpin all of higher education have been changing at an accelerating pace. Higher education is now in the early stages of an era that will have more significant revisions in academic structures, operations, and cultures than any period since the 1960s. By 2025, the face and character of higher education in the United States will have changed greatly, driven in part by new developments in several key areas—the economic model of education, the diversity of the student body, the nature of research and knowledge generation, the forms and modes of teaching and learning, the focus of external frameworks used to assess institutional performance, the criteria associated with institutional reputation and prestige—as well as by the introduction of a new generation of faculty who are already crafting a new academic culture.

Civic engagement will play a role in how higher education adapts to all of these changes and to other important trends in society, in the United States and around the world. Contemporary pressures to make undergraduate learning more efficient, rapid, and competency-based are challenging many institutions to be more intentional about all aspects of student learning and development. Similar pressures call for research to be more interdisciplinary, collaborative, networked, and focused on the "Big Questions." In this rapidly changing environment, attention to community engagement is a beneficial institutional strategy because engaged practices align with the new skills and approaches necessary to improve effectiveness in teaching, learning, and research.

Add to this context the emerging insights about the working styles, expectations, and values of a new generation of faculty entering higher education in ever larger numbers. Research reveals their strong desire for an academic culture that is interdisciplinary, collaborative, linked to contemporary questions, and enacted through a blended approach to teaching, research, and service.[1] Many newer faculty members participated in service learning or other civic learning activities in their own high school or undergraduate development. As more of these Gen X and Y faculty enter the academy and move into leadership and governance roles, we will see growing support for an intentional, integrated, strategic agenda that frames community and civic engagement as a force for integrating the forms of scholarship, as Ernest Boyer predicted in 1990.[2] Institutions will need to innovate and adapt to these new expectations, acting with greater attention and intentionality as they implement and evaluate civic learning and engagement actions and strategies—not just for the sake of documentation or to justify internal support, but to improve quality and impact for campuses and communities and to promote collaboration and sustained agendas of engagement that lead to new outcomes for students and the community.

THE NEED FOR INTENTIONAL MONITORING AND MEASURING OF CIVIC LEARNING AND TEACHING

A focus on more systematic, comprehensive, and ongoing monitoring and evaluation of civic learning activities and outcomes creates the opportunity to address long-standing questions about civic engagement's effects on students, community partners, faculty, and academic institutions, and the relationships among these effects. Example questions include the following:

- What components of, or strategies for, civic engagement activities lead to successful learning outcomes for students and meet the goals of communities?
- How do students affect communities with their presence and actions?
- Do different models of civic learning align with similar or different specific learning outcomes?
- How does interaction with communities contribute to student learning and development?
- What is the community's role in civic learning activities, and what are the costs and benefits of the community's efforts?
- Under what conditions does engaged teaching lead faculty to develop new lines of research?
- To what degree should civic learning be intentionally organized into pathways of developmental learning, or woven throughout the institution in a way that makes the civic mission and experience pervasive?

The answers to these and many similar questions could inform a new, more intentional and coherent approach to civic learning and engagement—one that clarifies and strengthens the roles and contributions of students, faculty, and community members as they work together on civic topics and issues. Such a clarification and blending of roles may lead to several important next-stage developments in the practices of civic teaching and learning, and may also enrich and deepen our understanding of civic engagement and partnerships.

For example, attention to mutually beneficial outcomes for all participants (students, community members, faculty) in any campus-community partnership has always been at the heart of every definition and form of civic engagement. Yet these activities sometimes tend to yield transactional outcomes rather than collaborative agendas that would generate shared and separate benefits for all involved.

In some cases, where a defined task is the primary focus of the partnership, insufficient attention to mutual benefit can make it seem as if the students and the community partner are traveling in parallel universes, working together in the moment and then parting from each other to consider what came of the interaction from their two different perspectives. Attention to quality practice and outcomes, monitored and measured systematically over time, can bring rich learning and knowledge exchange, even in transactional partnerships.

In order to frame an ongoing agenda for interaction going forward, effective approaches to organizing civic learning programs and community partnerships will need to better reflect an intentional alignment of institutional goals and strengths with community issues and opportunities. In this model, students, faculty, campus leaders, and community partners would all be aware of each other's agendas and goals, and thus better able to monitor progress, adapt approaches, and capture outcomes from both an academic and a community perspective. Each party would know their role, their opportunities to learn, their expected outcomes, and how all of these things would be measured. A more intentional, co-designed, and sustained agenda of civic work shared between academia and communities has the potential to create a landscape of activity that can be monitored, improved, or adapted as work progresses, with outcomes that can be evaluated or measured across all participants.

What Makes the Assessment of Inclusive Civic Learning and Teaching So Difficult?

Given that higher education is a knowledge-driven enterprise, it is puzzling that so many academics and administrators seem so averse to evaluation and measurement of their own academic activities. When conducting workshops on monitoring and measuring community engagement, as I have done with growing frequency over the last several years, I often lighten the atmosphere by asking participants to raise their hands if they will admit that when writing a grant proposal, they usually leave the evaluation plan section as the last thing to do because they really hate doing it. Many hands go up in response to this question, accompanied by blushing and giggling. This reluctance has many causes, but often reflects confusion about what ought to be evaluated in activities like civic learning that involve diverse participants and complex factors and contexts.

Many practitioners and mid-level organizational leaders engaged in civic learning and teaching concentrate their energy and enthusiasm on designing and implementing the work, on assessing student outcomes, and sometimes on collecting feedback from community partners. Yet when data are needed, senior staff may assign the task of measurement to these same individuals, some of whom may have done excellent research and evaluation of their projects and programs, while others may not have the skills, time, or resources to do so. The long neglect of this issue of measurement seems partly rooted in a tradition of making the case for civic learning and teaching by appealing to a vision of the work as inherently good and valuable, with the hope that it will earn support and recognition through what advocates often see as its obvious merit. Simply said, it is easier and more appealing to make the case for institutional support by telling individual stories of student and community impact than it is to design formal measurement tools that gather information on outcomes across the diverse forms and goals of civic learning and teaching. That said, many individual or specific civic learning and teaching activities and programs have high-quality embedded strategies for measurement, assessment, or evaluation. These individual, small program evaluations are often the source of data for much of the extant literature. A broader, systematic approach for monitoring and measuring activity and outcomes across a whole institution is rare.

To some degree, early attention to a more analytical examination of civic learning and teaching activities arose from the desire of advocates for greater institutional support. These advocates saw monitoring the scope and range of what individual institutions were actually doing as a way of describing progress and inferring value for further investment, yielding a path toward institutionalizing a commitment to civic learning and teaching, including service learning and partnerships. Early assessment instruments were designed to describe civic learning and teaching activities (with their many different names and forms) and their distribution, goals, practices, and strategies. Thus most of these instruments relied on descriptive data rather than on measurement or assessment of short-term or long-term outcomes.

Early encouragement for institutions to take a detailed look at their comprehensive portrait of civic learning came from specific frameworks such as Campus Compact's national survey of its members, the Learn and Serve America grantee survey, and Andy Furco's Self-Assessment Rubric for Institutionalizing Service Learning in Higher Education.[3] A real strength and contribution of these and similar tools—which aimed to track or encourage institutionalization—was their ability to reinforce institutional language, terminology, and principles of good practice relating to civic learning, teaching, and partnerships. Yet those staff and faculty who worked to complete or apply these instruments found that the very nature of civic engagement made it easier to focus on collecting descriptive information about what was happening across an institution rather than to focus on collecting data about the outcomes of the activity. Civic engagement, learning, and teaching are based on relationships among students, instructors, and community partners. Their learning and developmental outcomes are complex, challenging, and expressed in diverse ways by students. The design of learning activities and the consequential interactions among students, instructors, and partners are highly diverse and difficult to compare. Language has long been a point of difference and dispute: for example, "service learning" is a common term with well-established techniques and design principles, and it may be used as a strategy to facilitate student acquisition of a wide spectrum of student learning goals including civic learning. However, these two terms can be confusing; many would argue that "service learning" and "civic learning" have different meanings and are different learning models. Others would say that service learning is a method and civic learning is a goal of service learning. Such variability in use of terms (and of activity designs) makes monitoring and measurement within and across institutions a challenge.

Another challenge arises from the extended effect of civic learning experiences. Impacts and outcomes of any form of civic learning may not be obvious in the moment of the work itself, and may emerge later through reflection or additional experience. One of the most respected early works that illustrated the challenges of assessing civic learning outcomes or community outcomes was Eyler and Giles's *Where's the Learning in Service-Learning?*[4] In this work, the authors identified the diversity of forms, goals, strategies, and contexts across different civic learning activities and settings as a major barrier to large-scale or consistent analysis of learning outcomes. The literature on civic learning methods and outcomes has grown continuously over the last fifteen years, but most assessment efforts continue to focus on small groups or projects, and the limitations that Eyler and Giles explained so clearly continue to persist as barriers to large-scale research or evaluation studies.

NEW OPPORTUNITIES AND MOTIVATIONS FOR
MONITORING AND MEASURING CIVIC LEARNING
Despite these challenges, a few developments have raised the profile of monitoring and measuring civic learning and teaching as a priority for strengthening shared outcomes for multiple constituencies going forward.

First, new recognition programs that offer national acknowledgement for civic teaching and learning have inspired institutions to gather data on their civic work. Prominent among these are the President's Higher Education Community Service Honor Roll and the Carnegie Elective Classification for Community Engagement. In 2013, nearly six hundred colleges and universities were included in the President's Community Service Honor Roll, which asks institutions to provide mostly quantitative data about student service and volunteering and the purposes of these activities. The program has four levels of recognition and is designed to acknowledge higher education's role in community problem solving through activities that are also meant to develop civic responsibility in students. Given that every institution has many student volunteering organizations, days of service, and other student- and institution-led activities that involve extracurricular and curricular service, the task of getting accurate data is huge and presents challenges to all applicants for the Honor Roll. For institutions that seek to earn, retain, or achieve a higher level of recognition for this annual award, there is considerable incentive to build more routine and ongoing systems for collecting data rather than, as many institutions often do, cobble data together each year on an ad hoc basis.

The Carnegie Elective Classification for Community Engagement, now managed by the New England Resource Center for Higher Education (NERCHE), has a completely different purpose from the Honor Roll. It requires very different kinds of information and has a different and important impact on attention to an integrated view of evaluating engagement, including civic learning strategies. The Carnegie Classification is not an award, but a "process of self-assessment and quality improvement."[5] The Carnegie tool aims to capture a comprehensive snapshot of community engagement across an institution, including in elements of the institutional mission, leadership, community involvement and feedback, curriculum, faculty rewards, research, campus-community partnerships, and public service and outreach, among others. Each institution completes an individual application, which NERCHE staff review without comparison to or ranking among other applicants and without requiring that specific thresholds or quantitative indicators be met. The Carnegie form is designed to prompt applicant institutions to describe and reflect on elements of their community engagement in the context of elements of good practice. In assessing an institution's application, reviewers also consider the depth and sustainability of each case in the context of the institution's mission and aims. The information provided by applicants is largely descriptive but also includes some quantitative and analytical data, as well as examples of relevant documents or policies that reflect the institution's specific actions that support deeper achievement of its civic mission.

The Carnegie Classification has had a high-profile impact on institutional commitment to creating systematic mechanisms for collecting data and documentation on an ongoing basis. The application process was run in 2006, 2008, and 2010 and has now moved to a five-year cycle. Beginning with the current cycle of applicants, who will receive results of their applications in 2015, previously classified institutions will reapply on a ten-year cycle. Substantial effort is required to complete the robust application process, and the application schedule gives institutions nearly two years to complete their submissions. Though the classification is not framed as an award, some institutions see it as such, and those institutions that have achieved classification are eager to retain it. Thus, the process's reputation for improving institutional performance regarding community engagement through self-reflection and data collection has inspired considerable national (and even international) interest in creating ongoing data collection or evaluation systems that will facilitate sustained reporting. This is an important outcome to note, because it appears that the Carnegie process is demonstrating a positive relationship between institutional intentionality and the ability or capacity to create a reasonably accurate and sustainable system for monitoring and measuring civic activities. Clearly, the Carnegie Classification experience has required institutions to develop more intentional approaches to civic and community engagement, and has encouraged more coherent approaches to the roles and relationships between students, faculty, campus leadership, and community leadership. For applicants who take the process seriously and take an institution-wide approach to gathering and interpreting their engagement stories, the classification encourages a greater melding of the roles of the different constituencies in civic learning, and will continue to do so.

A second influence resulting in rising attention to monitoring and measuring civic engagement comes from the various higher education organizations that have raised the profile of this work as a valuable strategy for institutional improvement. The Civic Series in which this essay appears, along with more than ten years of civic learning funding given to campuses through competitive grants, has been organized and led by Bringing Theory to Practice. The Association of American Colleges and Universities (AAC&U) also has led practitioners in creating useful rubrics for the assessment of civic learning outcomes and has produced research studies and reports on the topic.[6] AAC&U's influence has also helped to make civic learning a major goal of Lumina Foundation's Degree Qualifications Profile.[7] Campus Compact has raised the profile of the strategic importance and value of civic learning and engagement nationally, and thirty-four state

Compact organizations offer grants and programs that engage students, faculty, and community partners in civic learning and development that has included analytical and evaluative elements. The American Association of State Colleges and Universities (AASCU) has advocated for civic engagement since its 2002 report *Stepping Forward as Stewards of Place*, which summarized a national survey of its members that captured data on civic learning and engagement activities.[8] AASCU's American Democracy Project has also funded civic learning activities at many institutions, organized national conferences on civic learning, and encouraged measurement of civic learning outcomes.

These national projects and associations and others have done much to make civic engagement and learning more visible to higher education leaders—decision makers who encourage more intentional agendas of engagement across their own institutions. These organizations have also contributed to a wider interest in recognition programs and data collection, as well as to the growing understanding of how civic engagement benefits institutional priorities such as student recruitment, campus diversity, student retention, enhanced research opportunities, and enhanced alumni and donor programs, among others. One indicator of how much the profile of civic and community engagement has grown is that almost all regional accrediting bodies now incorporate standards related to this work.

A third force resulting in greater focus on measurement and evaluation is the attention that societies and networks are now giving to civic engagement and learning. Entities like Project Kaleidoscope have begun to integrate civic learning into research initiatives linked to STEM learning, sustainability, diversity, and global learning outcomes. Some disciplinary societies have begun offering conference tracks related to engaged teaching and research. The Talloires Network has made civic learning a topic of dialogue, action, and exchange among networks of engaged universities in eight regions of the world. The International Association for Research on Service-Learning and Community Engagement (IARSLCE), which grew out of a conference held in 2001, has created a global platform for disseminating peer-reviewed research on all dimensions and interpretations of civic and community engagement across the spectrum of higher education. IARSLCE has attracted more than four hundred individual members from more than thirty nations and is deeply committed to the mentoring of graduate students as future engaged scholars and civic teachers.

STRATEGIES FOR MONITORING AND MEASURING CIVIC LEARNING
AND TEACHING ON CAMPUSES

Recently, interest in strategies for evaluating civic learning projects to capture outcomes data has increased intensely. Unfortunately, this has led to a mindset of searching for the 'One Tool,' with some expecting to find a cookbook that they can hand out to faculty, partners, or students. Such simplicity belies the core complexity of civic learning and engagement as a form of scholarship and as a method of teaching, learning, research, and collaboration with other entities that promotes positive change in communities. Civic learning and teaching is scholarly work grounded in relationships, negotiation of mutual benefits, attention to reciprocity, and appropriately different perspectives on the outcomes sought. Given the national and international attention to the need for more systematic mechanisms to monitor, measure, and evaluate civic learning and engagement, what approaches are colleges and universities using to enhance our collective understanding of the models and outcomes generated through knowledge-driven interactions among students, community, and faculty?

The first step toward greater understanding is for colleges and universities to clearly define and distinguish the terms: monitoring, measuring, and evaluating. They are not interchangeable.

Monitoring involves a focus on *what is going on*. Many institutional leaders or civic teachers say that "we need to measure civic engagement" when they are really talking about capturing the landscape of activity. Because civic learning activities happen at random on many campuses, it is not surprising that few institutions fully grasp the array of their civic learning and teaching efforts. In my view, there is great value in focusing first on capturing an accurate portrait of engagement within each institution. Without identifying the specific body of work or range of activities that are relevant to civic learning and engagement, how would one know what to measure or evaluate? Driven in part by the President's Honor Roll and the Carnegie application process, many colleges and universities focus initially and even primarily on creating strategies to inventory civic learning and other community engagement activities across campus. There are several basic approaches to such a process: an annual survey of all faculty (and often staff); a permanent database with records created and maintained by individual faculty, staff, or students; or a hybrid approach that draws information from a mix of existing surveys, annual faculty activity reports, departmental meetings or interviews, as well as data sets kept by student affairs, human resources, the research/grants administrative unit, the institutional research office, the registrar, or other units.

A good monitoring strategy typically yields information about each civic activity's leaders; participants; external partners; purpose and location; connection to teaching, learning, and research or public service and outreach; the civic issues and community populations it addresses; and its strategy for addressing these issues and populations. Faculty and staff in charge of many existing civic learning and teaching activities may already have conducted high-quality assessments or formal evaluations of outcomes achieved by faculty, students, and community partners. This is why monitoring schemes are so valuable: they focus on collecting the considerable assessment and evaluation data that is often already available.

If monitoring is about what is going on, then *measurement* is about *what happened* as a result. An effective monitoring system provides a foundation of descriptive information that makes it possible to contact community partners, students, and faculty and collect information and feedback from them; to convene faculty and partners working on similar issues or in similar areas; or to identify needs for faculty development to improve existing efforts or create opportunities for replication. A good monitoring system allows faculty and staff to analyze this descriptive information to capture inputs and outputs, which are not unimportant. Strong input and output measures indicate the level of activity across the institution, reveal gaps or opportunities for improvement and replication, and point to areas that might benefit from collaboration, infrastructure, or resources. Measuring involves taking the inputs (e.g., resources, forms of different activities and projects, identity of participants, etc.) and outputs (e.g., the scope, scale, location, purpose and products of those activities) identified through the monitoring process, and then analyzing them further to identify *patterns* across activities and projects, and the *intended/achieved outcomes* for each constituency. Is there a lot of civic learning in the first year but not much in the second year? Are there rich opportunities in some disciplines but fewer in others? Are a few faculty members responsible for a significant percentage of civic learning activities? Where are there opportunities to bring together multiple projects that have common factors such as similar community partners or issues, similar learning goals, etc.? What is the pattern of intended outcomes for students and for partners? What types of deliverables, new funds, or new research outcomes have resulted from the activities? Exploration of the answers to these questions is of great value. While mainly resulting in descriptive data, the monitoring process can inform analysis and planning of future faculty development opportunities, recognition programs, and strategies for program improvement or replication of successful models of civic learning and partnerships. A good monitoring system can also capture the institution's overall civic learning story, which can be shared both internally and externally for improvement and recognition as well as for fund-raising purposes.

Measuring also involves collecting feedback from each of the constituent groups in civic learning and teaching—the students, the faculty, and the community. Each of these groups has unique goals, expectations, responsibilities, and skills to bring to the collaborative activity and partnership. Thus, although a common tool or strategy can be used to gather data from each constituent group, efforts to capture feedback and measure outcomes must be distinct for each.[9] When civic learning occurs as a component of the curriculum, student data come first and foremost from classroom assessments of learning. Student outcomes also can be collected through questions added to course evaluations, exit surveys at the end of one-time events, analysis of reflection activities, and unique course or program surveys. When assessing student learning, some institutions ask community partners to contribute input. Data from faculty can be gathered through the monitoring strategy described above, through focus groups among practitioners of civic teaching, or through annual surveys, using instruments designed to capture outputs that reflect the institution's goals for civic learning and teaching. For example, a faculty survey may capture outcomes by asking respondents to list academic or nonacademic publications and presentations or by requiring them to answer questions about the impact of the community partner relationship on their scholarly or service agenda. By facilitating the collection of community partners' contact information, a good monitoring strategy can lay the groundwork for the distribution of feedback surveys among community partners. These surveys can include questions about partnership practices, partner satisfaction, communications between the community partner and the institution, costs and benefits, and partners' views of outcomes.

However, research shows that most partners prefer to provide feedback in focus groups, in part because they value the opportunity to hear from each other and also strengthen their relationship with the academic institution beyond their specific faculty partner.[10]

As illustrated above, measuring involves analyzing the institution's civic learning practices and performance, and the results can be used in many ways, internally and externally. *Evaluation* is a formal enterprise aimed at examining the quality of an activity or program design, and it involves conducting a formal and systematic study to determine the presence or absence of specific outcomes. Evaluation of civic learning, and other engagement activities or partnership projects, involves gathering evidence to analyze each activity or project's design, implementation, and intended goals or outcomes. Most evaluation studies in the literature are based on single activities or projects, which is not a bad thing when civic learning activities involve different methods, goals, partners, or intended outcomes. As more colleges and universities become more strategic and intentional in their approach to community partnerships and civic learning strategies, larger scale evaluations of similar programs and/or similar intended outcomes will be possible. For example, an institution that has a number of civic partnerships focused on literacy among recent immigrants could conduct a formal evaluation of all these programs to capture outcomes and identify any patterns or findings that might shed light on the effectiveness of different interventions or program design strategies. Evaluations require funding, but when focused on civic learning or engagement, they can also help generate external revenue. Donors and other entities concerned about civic literacy will likely be interested in supporting the work of an academic institution that demonstrates a sustained commitment to the topic.

To some degree, the growing pressure to produce data has impeded the ability of civic learning leaders on campuses to recognize existing data sources already embedded in learning and teaching activities and assessments, to carefully interpret and apply the existing data, and to compose thoughtful questions aligned with the goals of data collection. What do we really seek to know about how students affect communities? Are we prepared to discover that students' civic engagement activities actually have few cumulative effects in the community, having been designed to serve student learning goals more than to create real change in society? Are we prepared to discover that we may be serving mostly students who already are civically minded and socially responsible, while often failing to reach students who are less engaged?

Our desire to gather data may actually require us to explore a deeper question: To what end do we seek to measure and evaluate? We may find that we measure only to make a case for internal support, when it would be better to measure in order to improve the work, build collaboration, and magnify the effects of civic learning activities for all participating constituencies, so as to create real progress in addressing the "Big Questions." Through monitoring and evaluation, institutions are becoming able to better recognize the contributions community partners make to civic teaching and learning, the contributions students make to community capacity, and the benefits to the academic institution's larger strategic goals as an engaged college or university. Without intentionally taking an ongoing and systematic approach, institutions will continue to find that their civic engagement efforts involve largely random participation and result in random outcomes.

SUMMARY

Higher education around the world is changing fast as the result of powerful internal and external pressures and following the natural course of generational change. Civic learning and engagement not only affects those who participate in it, but also serves as a valuable tool for helping institutions adapt more quickly to new expectations and conditions. Institutions can gain performance advantages by intentionally adopting an agenda of civic learning and teaching, developing a more focused approach to working with external partners, and integrating that work intentionally into a spectrum of teaching, learning, and research activities. These activities must be monitored and measured to ensure improvement and effectiveness, and to promote collaboration and impact. An emphasis on systematic monitoring and measuring is essential to sustainability, impact, and quality. The more we emphasize attention to outcomes, the more we will understand that civic learning and teaching are about high-quality partnerships and civic learning models that benefit students, faculty, and communities. Through measurement and learning assessment, we will learn more about collaboration, more easily recognize and honor the contributions community partners make to student learning and development, and more fully be able to describe the contributions students make to community change.

Ultimately, we need a national database on civic learning and teaching—not to bolster institutional reputations or to foster competition, but to track the level and types of civic activities across campuses and to compare the different approaches to working in partnership with communities. Such a database could lead to regional and national collaborations that substantially improve community capacity and conditions, as well as civic learning for students. Going forward, there is likely to be greater attention to research, learning, and teaching models that align the goals of higher education and other community sectors to generate co-created knowledge. Thus, civic learning strategies will contribute to the realization of Gibbons et al. in their description of the concept of transdisciplinary scholarship, and of Boyer's vision for a more integrated view of scholarly work that links learning with discovery in ways that contribute to public or community purposes.[11]

Greater attention to capturing and analyzing the results of civic learning and teaching will help higher education evolve, as it must, into a sector characterized by cooperation rather than competition—a sector that is prepared to respond to the large-scale problems that challenge our nation and the world. Addressing such issues is the true purpose of the scholarly enterprise, and it should be the ultimate aim of our commitment to monitoring, measuring, and evaluating civic learning and teaching. At the same time, it will also serve the purposes of improving the quality of civic learning methods and deepening community-campus partnerships to enrich outcomes for all involved.

NOTES

1. Cathy Trower, "Gen X Meets Theory X: What New Scholars Want," *Journal of Collective Bargaining in the Academy* 0, article 11 (May 8, 2012).

2. Ernest Boyer, *Scholarship Reconsidered: Priorities of the Professoriate* (Princeton: Carnegie Foundation for the Advancement of Teaching, 1990).

3. See Campus Compact, *2012 Annual Membership Survey: Creating a Culture of Assessment* (Boston: Campus Compact, 2012). http://www.compact.org/about/statistics; Andrew Furco, "Self-Assessment Rubric for Institutionalizing Service Learning in Higher Education," (Berkeley, CA: University of California, Berkeley, 2002), http://talloiresnetwork.tufts.edu/wp-content/uploads/Self-AssessmentRubricfortheInstitutionalizationofService-LearninginHigherEducation.pdf; and Learn and Serve America Program and Performance Reporting System (LASSIE), http://www.reginfo.gov/public/do/PRAViewIC?ref_nbr=201006-3045-005&icID=29326.

4. Janet Eyler and Dwight E. Giles, *Where's the Learning in Service-Learning?* (San Francisco: Jossey-Bass, 1999).

5. Carnegie Foundation for the Advancement of Teaching, "Classification Description: Community Engagement Elective Classification," http://classifications.carnegiefoundation.org/descriptions/community_engagement.php.

6. See National Task Force on Civic Learning and Democratic Engagement, *A Crucible Moment: College Learning and Democracy's Future* (Washington, DC: Association of American Colleges and Universities, 2012); Greater Expectations National Panel, *Greater Expectations: A New Vision for Learning as a Nation Goes to College* (Washington, DC: Association of American Colleges and Universities, 2002); and the AAC&U VALUE rubrics at http://www.aacu.org/value/index.cfm.

7. Carol Geary Schneider, president of AAC&U, coauthored *The Degree Qualifications Profile* with Cliff Adelman, Peter Ewell, and Paul Gaston (Indianapolis: Lumina Foundation for Education, 2011).

8. American Association of State Colleges and Universities, *Stepping Forward as Stewards of Place* (Washington, DC: American Association of State Colleges and Universities, 2002), http://www.aascu.org/WorkArea/DownloadAsset.aspx?id=5458.

9. Sherril B. Gelmon, Barbara A. Holland, Amy Driscoll, Amy Spring, and Seanna Kerrigan, *Assessing Service-Learning and Civic Engagement: Principles and Techniques* (Providence, RI: Campus Compact, 2001).

10. Marie Sandy and Barbara A. Holland, "Different Worlds and Common Ground: Community Partner Perspectives on Campus-Community Partnerships," *Michigan Journal of Community Service Learning* 13, no. 1 (Fall 2006): 30–43.

11. Michael Gibbons, Camille Limoges, Helga Nowotny, Simon Schwartzman, Peter Scott, and Martin Trow, *The New Production of Knowledge* (Thousand Oaks, CA: Sage, 1994); Boyer, *Scholarship Reconsidered.*

4

Intergroup Dialogue and Civic and Service Learning: Toward Mutually Engaged Learning

Patricia Gurin and Biren (Ratnesh) A. Nagda

The most important impact of intergroup dialogue courses on my work now are the skills that I gained through practicing dialogue in conflict and in community. I find that leaders are more often distinguished by their interpersonal skills than by their technical knowledge, even where technical knowledge is a prerequisite to leadership. What interpersonal skills did intergroup dialogue teach me? I learned to find my own equanimity amid storms of conflict—to pause before responding and act with greater awareness and intention—to see patterns in my thoughts and feelings and the thoughts and feelings of people with different perspectives. I learned that the social good requires more than good intentions; it requires understanding the people around me and how my actions and the structure of our society impact their experience.
—AARON JAMES[1]

AARON JAMES, a graduate of the University of Michigan, wrote the comments above in response to questions we sent (in connection with a book we were writing, *Dialogue Across Difference*) to former undergraduate intergroup dialogue leaders pursuing careers in business, medicine, social work, public health, the arts, education, and law. Aaron now works in impact investing, where he helps people and organizations in rural communities connect with urban capital in the form of both philanthropic gifts and for-profit investments. He writes that, along with helping him build interpersonal skills, the intergroup dialogue work he did during college helped him develop social sensitivity—an awareness of his own and others' social identities and how they are embedded in cultural, political, and economic experiences. That lens now sharpens his perception of the separation between urban and rural communities, helping him recognize rural communities' heightened poverty and unemployment rates, and motivating his efforts to bond with rural residents at a level not often attempted by their urban counterparts.

The connection between what Aaron learned in his undergraduate intergroup dialogue courses and his current community practice might seem to imply a similar connection between intergroup dialogue and civic and service-learning courses. In fact, at most institutions, the two types of courses are not linked. Civic, service-learning, and community-based research courses do not usually include instruction in dialogue methods, and intergroup dialogue courses do not usually cover principles of community engagement. In 2014, students enrolled in a University of Michigan course designed to explore how integration could occur between the two types of courses confirmed that such mutuality is rare.[2] Through interviews with faculty and staff, the students revealed that instructors in only two of the ten community-based courses investigated used dialogue methods, while instructors in the ten intergroup dialogue courses studied did not ask students to apply dialogue in community settings, and did not typically cover community organizing principles and methods when helping students prepare to conduct action projects.

In this chapter, we propose a bridge between intergroup dialogue and civic and service-learning courses. Comparing and contrasting these courses' methods and learning outcomes, we suggest knowledge and skills that students should learn across both types of courses. These suggestions can guide efforts to create integrative courses and other methods of enhancing students' civic learning and democratic engagement.

INTERGROUP DIALOGUE

Intergroup dialogue, now offered through credit-bearing courses and short-term workshops at over 120 institutions,[3] is a distinct approach to surfacing the importance of group identities that are embedded in societal structures of power and privilege. Its *intergroup structure*—involving two identity groups with different experiences of power and privilege in society and sometimes on campus (for example, white students and students of color, Arab and Jewish students, first-generation students and students whose parents have college or post-graduate education, gay and straight students)—distinguishes it from approaches like deliberative dialogue. In deliberative dialogue, people from many different backgrounds (of race, ethnicity, socioeconomic status, etc.) come together around a community problem or issue of shared interest; however, the dialogue's structure promotes discussion within the group as a whole instead of emphasizing identity-based experiences and perspectives.[4] In contrast, in intergroup dialogue, social identities and shared group experiences and perspectives are always central to the learning process.

Students from different groups that have been advantaged and disadvantaged by social stratification in the United States come to intergroup dialogue with different orientations. Recent research in social psychology shows that people from more and less privileged groups bring different motivations to intergroup contact.[5] People from more privileged groups want to focus on learning about individuals rather than groups, to discover and emphasize commonalities rather than differences, and to look for individualized solutions to shared problems or for consensual approaches to action. People from less privileged groups likewise want to get to know individuals in the other group, but they also want to deal explicitly with group experiences, to discuss how power and privilege affect the two groups, and to look for collective as well as individual solutions. Researchers have observed these different orientations in contact situations involving Palestinians and Israeli Jews in Israel, and Catholics and Protestants in Northern Ireland.[6] The analytic framework that places group experiences, including those deriving from the structures and dynamics of power and privilege, at the center of participants' learning makes intergroup dialogue a social justice approach to education.

Since the inception of intergroup dialogue in the late 1980s, intergroup dialogue facilitators have sought to help students understand and work with intergroup conflicts—not only those that are historical and structural in nature, but also those that are persistent and present in their daily lives. The aims of intergroup dialogue include helping students gain knowledge of group-based social identities and inequalities; helping students improve and deepen intergroup communication and relationships; and helping students develop skills in and commitment to collaborations that do not ignore or minimize the different action orientations that students from different identity groups may hold.[7] Evidence from a nine-university experimental study supports the impact of intergroup dialogue on intergroup understanding, relationships, and collaboration.[8]

The effects of intergroup dialogue result from its distinctive pedagogy—integrating content learning, structured interactions, and facilitative guidance—and the communication processes this pedagogy encourages. Some of these processes are dialogic in the sense that they help students learn to listen to each other, to probe and follow up on each other's ideas, and to share perspectives and experiences. Other processes are critical in an analytic sense, as they help students learn to think critically about inequality, power, and privilege and to build alliances based on understanding rather than ignoring group differences.[9] Students engage in both dialogic and critical processes through individual reflection papers, interactive educational activities, and especially through collective reflection and dialogue to derive learning at the end of each dialogue class session.

We believe that instruction in intergroup understanding, the dynamics of intergroup relationships, and the elements of intergroup collaboration should be part of civic learning and community engagement courses. Furthermore, the collective reflection and sense-making in dialogues can also deepen civic and service learning. These elements can help prepare students working in communities to grasp how the different groups they encounter may view problems, issues, and solutions in different ways.

CIVIC AND SERVICE LEARNING

Early versions of civic education focused on teaching students about the various branches of local, state, and federal government and the basic facts of US history. Today, however, many educators conceive of civic and service learning much more broadly. For example, in *A Crucible Moment: College Learning and Democracy's Future,* the National Task Force on Civic Learning and Democratic Engagement stresses that students "need to understand the cultural and global contexts in which democracy is both deeply valued and deeply contested.... [Such] democratic knowledge and capabilities... are honed through hands on, face to face, active engagement in the midst of differing perspectives about how to address common problems that affect the well being of the nation and the world."[10] This broader view of civic learning includes knowledge, skills, values, and the capacity to work with others.

Civic and service learning courses typically involve active participation in thoughtfully organized service that is conducted in and meets the needs of a community. Ideally, civic and service-learning practices enhance the academic curriculum, and thus differ from volunteer experiences in community settings. These practices constitute an instructional strategy to meet learning goals.[11] In civic and service-learning courses, students practice their academic learning through internships in community agencies and other group settings. Reflection is a widely used learning mechanism in civic and service-learning courses to ensure that students recognize and internalize what they are learning within the classroom and through community work.

COMMONALITIES AND DIFFERENCES ACROSS INTERGROUP DIALOGUE
AND CIVIC AND SERVICE LEARNING

With different histories and structural locations within higher education, we might expect to find few commonalities across intergroup dialogue and civic and service-learning courses. However, despite these differences, we observe a number of commonalities across these two sets of courses in learning outcomes and methods of learning.

Learning Outcomes

Intergroup dialogue courses and civic and service learning courses have multiple similarities in learning outcomes. Both sets of courses emphasize knowledge of diverse cultures and religions in the United States and around the world; critical inquiry and reasoning capacities; collaborative capacities in decision-making and action; open mindedness and the capacity to engage different points of view; experience with diverse partners; and civility, ethical integrity, and mutual respect.[12]

However, the two types of courses have several differences in learning outcomes as well. Civic and service learning courses focus more than intergroup dialogue courses on knowledge of US history, political structures, and core democratic principles; knowledge of the political systems that frame constitutional democracies; and knowledge of political levers for effecting change.[13] In contrast, intergroup dialogue courses focus more than civic and service-learning courses on knowledge of social identities and knowledge of group-based inequalities, power, and privilege.

Methods of Learning

In both sets of courses, students apply their classroom knowledge. In intergroup dialogue, students apply their knowledge through "intergroup collaboration projects," in which groups of four students carry out a campus-based project designed to illuminate some aspect of inequality. In civic and service-learning courses, students apply their knowledge through community practice. Both aim to help students acquire higher-order skills, including critical thinking, communication, writing, interpersonal effectiveness, the ability to collaborate across diverse perspectives, and confidence in being able to enact change.[14] Both emphasize reflection as a major learning method.[15]

However, there are key differences in learning methods as well. For example, intergroup dialogue courses emphasize the critical-dialogic communication process that occurs in the classroom as the method by which learning outcomes are achieved, while civic and service-learning courses emphasize actual practice in communities.[16] In addition, intergroup dialogue focuses on groups; it assumes that the people living in any community will fall into multiple demographic, power, and interest groups representing different perspectives on community life and community issues.[17] Here, the *inter*group structure distinguishes the approach used in intergroup dialogue from that of civic and service learning, which emphasizes the *whole* community or *whole* group structure. Third, social identity plays a larger role in intergroup dialogue courses than in civic and service-learning courses. Despite the fact that students' social identities may affect their group interactions and relationships with community members, explicit attention to these social identities is rare in civic and service-learning courses. One faculty member interviewed by students at the University of Michigan in 2014 reported that in a course she teaches where student teams work with community agencies in Detroit, inter- and intragroup dynamics are some of the biggest challenges she faces. She also noted her concern about white students' tendency to address their Detroit community partners from a position of white privilege instead of making an effort to understand the unique urban issues in which the partners are immersed. Despite these concerns, this faculty member does not cover identity theory in her course or introduce students to research on the role of identity in communication across difference and differential power.

With alignment between many learning outcomes and methods of learning, intergroup dialogue and civic and service-learning courses should and could be better integrated for maximal effectiveness

With alignment between many learning outcomes and methods of learning, intergroup dialogue and civic and service-learning courses should and could be better integrated for maximal effectiveness. What follows are possible ways for faculty to foster such integration.

INTEGRATION OF INTERGROUP DIALOGUE AND CIVIC/SERVICE LEARNING
Integration does not have to occur within a single course. Both intergroup dialogue and civic and service-learning courses are designed to help students acquire knowledge and skills that require time and practice to understand and internalize. To think about how integration might occur, whether in courses specifically designed to foster integration or in other ways, it may be helpful to examine what knowledge and skills students need to integrate intergroup dialogue and community practice. The students in the University of Michigan's 2014 exploratory course collectively categorized such knowledge and skills as follows.

- *Social justice, inequalities, and identities*
  Knowledge of income and wealth inequalities; critical thinking about social identities; skills for talking about inequalities in accessible ways and for talking with community members with different identities
- *Communication and group dynamics*
  Knowledge of group dynamics in groups and teams, models of leadership, and the role of social identities in collaboration across differences; skills

in active listening, asking questions, and probing multiple perspectives; facilitation skills

- *Community development/organization*
  Knowledge of principles and theories of organizational development, public and private for-profit and non-profit organizations, and multiple cultures within a community; skills in entering and exiting a community, assessing community needs, and building relationships with community agencies and community members; knowledge of the role of students' and community members' identities in collaboration
- *Research*
  Knowledge of methods of community-based research and of community needs assessment; skills in creating assessment tools collaboratively with community agencies and members, in collecting and analyzing data, and in reporting and discussing findings with community members; skills in using dialogue in community research relationships; skills in grant writing
- *Student development*
  Knowledge of theories of student development; knowledge of connections between dialogue and community experience; skills related to problem solving across differences, critical thinking, and planning and organizing; practice in flexibility and openness to multiple perspectives

How might such knowledge and skills be taught and acquired? There are many ways, of course; but in all cases, it is essential that faculty members work with community leaders and consultants to mutually create teaching plans that enable students' learning to align with community organizations' needs, and that allow community partners to participate in teaching. Although an academic institution's primary mission is educating its students, its collaboration with the communities in which it is embedded is also crucial. In endeavoring to integrate intergroup dialogue and civic and service learning, higher education institutions must function as "anchor institutions"—"being 'of their communities and not just in them.'"[18]

The four ideas for integrating intergroup dialogue and civic and service learning suggested below originated in conversations held by students in the 2014 University of Michigan course with faculty members and with community members and consultants in the Detroit, Michigan, area.[19]

1) *Workshops that help faculty and staff combine civic and service learning and intergroup dialogue in their courses.* Recognizing that many faculty and staff who currently teach courses in either intergroup dialogue or civic and service learning may lack the expertise necessary to cover the knowledge and skills generally acquired in the other area, institutions could offer workshops lasting one or two class sessions that faculty could incorporate into their existing courses. The students in the 2014 University of Michigan exploratory course suggested four such workshops, each with a similar format (an online tutorial with one or two readings covering basic concepts, followed by in-class work). Each workshop would include clear goals; learning exercises such as writing and collective reflection; and suggested readings and activities for students to advance their learning. The students proposed workshops focused on (a) the community context for learning and collaboration; (b) social identity

awareness and its influence on student–community collaboration; (c) communication and group dynamics in teams and in student–community relationships; and (d) models of community change and organizing.

2) *Mini-courses that build the foundation for subsequent intergroup dialogue and civic and service-learning courses.* More sustained than a one- or two-session workshop, mini-courses could offer the same content and the same in-class learning exercises but would also include visits with community organizations and a one-session retreat with community leaders. Students could enroll in mini-courses as preparation for intergroup dialogue and civic and service-learning courses. Each mini-course could provide one credit and last a few weeks, allowing students to learn both on campus and in (and with) the community.

3) *Capstone courses bringing together students from both intergroup dialogue and civic and service-learning courses.* A third idea focused on the later undergraduate years: a capstone course for students with two or more civic and service-learning courses and two or more intergroup dialogue courses (one of which should involve dialogue facilitation). The goal of the capstone course would be for students to share what they had learned in their respective courses, to discuss how to integrate the knowledge and skills they had gained across their courses, and to explore ways of continuing their learning and commitment to community development and change after leaving college.

4) *Graduate and professional school courses.* In many professional schools, students engage in community-based educational experiences where they work directly on community projects and with community groups and organizations. Courses using intergroup dialogue methods could be offered as supplements to these educational experiences. At the University of Washington, for example, students in advanced courses in social work take on the challenge of applying social justice principles to community action. Students often have prior knowledge of and education in social justice issues but feel stuck or uncertain about how to apply that knowledge to actual practice. A graduate-level course lays the foundation of intergroup dialogue as a community-centered practice (with a focus on building just relationships and just communities rather than simply critiquing and deconstructing power dynamics). The course engages students in reflecting on their field-based social work placements through a critical-dialogic lens—promoting critical reflection on their own identities as well as on their entry into and place within the community, encouraging them to understand intergroup relations and recognize power inequalities in their agencies and community settings, and helping them envision individual and collective leverage points for deepening dialogue, community, and social change action. Embracing a *praxis* approach to learning (combining reflection and action),[20] students work in diverse groups of four or five to reflect collectively on their field-based experiences, and to design and co-facilitate a dialogue for the whole class based on new questions emerging from their collective reflections. The larger classroom dialogue enables all students to engage deeply and meaningfully in individual and small-group deliberations about community practice and social justice, and to generatively apply emergent lessons directly to their practices in the community agencies.

CONCLUSION

While our two universities, the University of Washington and the University of Michigan, offer both long-term and ongoing opportunities for students to gain knowledge and skills in both intergroup dialogue and community practice, the integration of these experiences is generally left up to the students themselves. And many do it well.[21] We were much impressed by the specific examples of integration that graduates of our two intergroup dialogue programs described when writing for our book, *Dialogue Across Difference*.[22]

For example, Jaimée Marsh, a multiracial, multiethnic woman who graduated from both Universities of Washington and Michigan, is now the assistant director of the Q-Center at the University of Washington, where she uses her training in intergroup dialogue, community-based research, and international experiences to empower students to explore their social identities, to collaborate in social justice activities on campus and in the Seattle community, and to offer dialogue opportunities for students exploring sexual orientation and gender expression within both K–12 and university settings. She says that in her professional experience, her ability to leverage her own identities, experiences, and intercultural competencies has proved essential.

Another University of Washington graduate, Joshua Johnson, an African American community organizer, writes that he creates spaces for dialogue within the larger community. As a community organizer, he stresses the importance of being aware of how we relate to others on the basis of our multiple identities. He has found such awareness essential as he canvasses diverse neighborhoods and engages with different personalities, building power with hundreds of diverse people, and empowering them to affect the narrative of change in our country.

After graduating from the University of Michigan, Chloé Gurin-Sands, a multiracial and multiethnic woman, took a position with the University's Spectrum Center to work collaboratively with campus identity groups, especially groups of color that sometimes are not invited into campus-based LGBTQ initiatives. Now entering a master's degree program in public health, she will use her intergroup dialogue skills in her graduate university's new undergraduate dialogue program while continuing to apply her research and community organizing skills through internships with Latino/a and African American populations. She writes that intergroup dialogue helped her build knowledge about and ability to discuss identity-based oppression, and frame health issues in a social justice way.

Kartik Sidhar, a South Asian medical student who facilitated intergroup dialogue at the University of Michigan and collaborated in developing a new dialogue course on ability and disability, is motivated as a future health practitioner to address health disparities and improve doctor-patient relationships. In medical school, he has developed a four-session intergroup dialogue workshop for first- and second-year medical students to explore their social identities and how those identities may affect their relationships with other staff, patients, and community health professionals. Along with the director of medical education, he has written about this workshop and about faculty training in dialogic methods as part of a longitudinal case study describing his institution's practice of matching medical students with a family, usually from a cultural or economic background different from their own, to develop personal relationships and become health advocates for two years.[23]

Despite these successes, we believe that scholars and practitioners of intergroup dialogue and civic and service learning should not leave the integration of dialogue and community-based practice only to students themselves. Instead, these faculty and staff members should come together with community consultants to offer courses, workshops, and other educational approaches that will foster the integration necessary to enhance engaged learning on the campus and in the community. The challenges and opportunities for faculty and community partners are to envision and construct sustainable bridges between intergroup dialogue ("classroom as community") and civic and service learning ("community as classroom"). With university and community members working as true partners, students can develop not only knowledge and skills about social justice and action, but also ways of being in the classroom and in the community that are just and mutually beneficial, as well as educationally and practically impactful.

> *Scholars and practitioners of intergroup dialogue and civic and service learning should not leave the integration of dialogue and community-based practice only to students themselves*

Notes

1. The quoted material appears in an unpublished essay Aaron James provided during the research stages of Patricia Gurin, Biren (Ratnesh) A. Nagda, and Ximena Zúñiga, *Dialogue Across Difference: Practice, Theory, and Research on Intergroup Dialogue* (New York: Russell Sage Foundation, 2013).

2. This course was supported by a grant from the University of Michigan's provost as part of a new initiative to foster engaged learning. Sandra Gregerman and Jenna Steiner from the University Research Opportunity Program, Lorraine Gutierrez from the Detroit Initiative, and Kelly Maxwell, Susan King, and Patricia Gurin from the Program on Intergroup Relations were involved in the grant and in designing the course.

3. One hundred and twenty institutions have attended the National Institute on Intergroup Dialogue, offered annually at the University of Michigan.

4. Nicholas V. Longo, "Deliberative Pedagogy in the Community: Connecting Deliberative Dialogue, Community Engagement, and Democratic Education," *Journal of Public Deliberation* 9, no. 2 (2013): 1–18; Martha L. McCoy and Patrick L. Scully, "Deliberative Dialogue to Expand Civic Engagement: What Kind of Talk Does Democracy Need?" *National Civic Review* 91, no. 2 (2002): 117–35; Ximena Zúñiga and Biren (Ratnesh) A. Nagda, "Design Considerations for Intergroup Dialogue," in *Intergroup Dialogue: Deliberative Democracy in School, College, Community and Workplace*, ed. David Schoem and Sylvia Hurtado (Ann Arbor: University of Michigan Press, 2001), 306–327.

5. See, for example, Tamar Saguy, John F. Dovidio, and Felicia Pratto, "Beyond Contact: Intergroup Contact in the Context of Power Relations," *Personality and Social Psychology Bulletin* 34, no. 3 (2008): 432–45; Tamar Saguy, Linda R. Tropp, and Diala Hawi, "The Role of Group Power in Intergroup Contact," in *Advances in Intergroup Contact*, ed. Gordon Hodson and Miles Hewstone (New York: Psychology Press, 2013), 113–32.

6. For a discussion of Palestinians and Israeli Jews, see Ifat Maoz, "Intergroup Contact in Settings of Protracted Ethnopolitical Conflict," in *The Oxford Handbook of Social Psychology and Social Justice*, ed. Phillip Hammack (New York: Oxford University Press, forthcoming). For a discussion of

Catholics and Protestants in Northern Ireland, see Kevin Durrheim and John Dixon, "Intergroup Contact and the Struggle for Social Justice," *Oxford Handbook*, ed. Phillip Hammack. See also Biren (Ratnesh) A. Nagda, Anna Yeakley, Patricia Gurin, and Nicholas Sorensen, "Intergroup Dialogue: A Critical–Dialogic Model for Conflict Engagement," *The Oxford Handbook of Intergroup Conflict*, ed. Linda Tropp (Oxford: Oxford University Press, 2012), 210–28.

7. David Schoem, Sylvia Hurtado, Todd Sevig, Mark Chesler, and Stephen H. Sumida, "Intergroup Dialogue: Democracy at Work in Theory and Practice," in *Intergroup Dialogue: Deliberative Democracy in School, College, Community and Workplace*, ed. David Schoem and Sylvia Hurtado (Ann Arbor: University of Michigan Press, 2001), 1–21; Ximena Zúñiga, Biren (Ratnesh) A. Nagda, Mark Chesler, and Adena Cytron-Walker, *Intergroup Dialogue in Higher Education: Meaningful Learning about Social Justice*, ASHE Higher Education Report 32, no. 4 (San Francisco, CA: Jossey-Bass, 2007).

8. For a summary of this research, see Gurin, Nagda, and Zúñiga, *Dialogue Across Difference*.

9. Biren (Ratnesh) A. Nagda, "Breaking Barriers, Crossing Borders, Building Bridges: Communication Processes in Intergroup Dialogues," *Journal of Social Issues* 62, no. 3 (2006): 553–76.

10. National Task Force on Civic Learning and Democratic Engagement, *A Crucible Moment: College Learning and Democracy's Future* (Washington, DC: Association of American Colleges and Universities, 2012), 3.

11. Timothy D. Knapp and Bradley J. Fisher, "The Effectiveness of Service-Learning: It's Not Always What You Think," *Journal of Experiential Education* 3, no. 33 (2010): 208–24.

12. See, as cited in National Task Force, *A Crucible Moment*; Janet S. Eyler, Dwight E. Giles, Jr., Christine M. Stenson, and Charlene J. Gray, *At a Glance: What We Know about the Effects of Service-Learning on College Students, Faculty, Institutions and Communities, 1993–2000*, 3rd ed. (Nashville: Vanderbilt University, 2001); Ashley Finley, "A Brief Review of the Evidence on Civic Learning in Higher Education" (Washington, DC: Association of American Colleges and Universities, 2012); Sara M. Gallini and Barbara E. Moely, "Service-Learning and Engagement, Academic Challenge, and Retention," *Michigan Journal of Community Service Learning* 10, no. 1 (2003): 5–14. See also Gurin, Nagda, and Zúñiga, *Dialogue Across Difference*; Zúñiga, Nagda, Chesler, and Cytron-Walker, Intergroup Dialogue.

13. National Task Force, *A Crucible Moment*, 4.

14. Christine M. Cress, "Civic Engagement and Student Success: Leveraging Multiple Degrees of Achievement," *Diversity & Democracy* 15, no. 3 (2012): 2–4, 23; Gurin, Nagda, and Zúñiga, *Dialogue Across Difference*.

15. Robert Bringle and Julie Hatcher, "Reflection in Service-Learning: Making Meaning of Experience," *Educational Horizons* 77, no. 4 (Summer 1999): 179–85; Gurin, Nagda, and Zúñiga, *Dialogue Across Difference*.

16. For suggestions of how dialogue may be utilized in civic or service learning, see Ariane Hoy, "Linking High-Impact Learning with High-Impact Community Engagement," *Diversity & Democracy* 15, no. 3 (2012): 5–7.

17. Writing about study circles, Katherine Cramer Walsh notes that the people she interviewed had hugely discrepant experiences and views of living in the same city. *Talking about Race: Community Dialogues and the Politics of Difference* (Chicago: University of Chicago Press, 2007).

18. Nancy Cantor, "A Map of Opportunity: Anchor Institutions and the Diverse Next Generation" (lecture, University of Southern California Enrollment Center: The Nexus of Mission, Excellence, and Diversity, Los Angeles, January 15, 2014).

19. Credit belongs to Amber Gustafson, Allie Harte, Kiven Lewis, Elizabeth Miller, Jasmayne Morgan, Dahlia Petrus, and Nicholas Renkes.

20. Paulo Freire, *Pedagogy of the Oppressed* (New York: Continuum, 1993).

21. See Ande Diaz and Rachael Perrault, "Sustained Dialogue and Civic Life: Post-College Impacts," *Michigan Journal of Community Service Learning* 17, no. 1 (2010): 32–43; Carolyn Vasques-Scalera, "Changing Facilitators, Facilitating Change: The Lives of Intergroup Dialogue Facilitators Post-College," in *Facilitating Intergroup Dialogues: Bridging Differences, Catalyzing Change*, ed. Kelly E. Maxwell, Biren (Ratnesh) A. Nagda, and Monita C. Thompson (Sterling, VA: Stylus Publishing, 2011), 201–12.

22. Gurin, Nagda, and Zúñiga, *Dialogue Across Difference*.

23. See Arno K. Kumagai and Monica L. Lypson, "Beyond Cultural Competence: Critical Consciousness, Social Justice, and Multicultural Education," *Academic Medicine* 84, no. 6 (2009): 782–87; and Katherine Bakke, Kartik Sidhar, and Arno K. Kumagai, "Virtual Mentor: Racism, Dialogue, Medical Education" (unpublished paper, Departments of Internal Medicine and Medical Education, University of Michigan Medical School, Ann Arbor, Michigan, 2013).

5 Blurring the Roles of Scientist and Activist through Citizen Science

Christina P. Colon and John Rowden

THE PURPOSE OF THIS CHAPTER is to promote the use of citizen science as a highly effective paradigm for civic engagement in the higher education biology class. While teaching bioethics has long been an important philosophical aspect of teaching biology, with science increasingly central to many political, social, economic, and environmental issues, and with professionals in science, technology, engineering, and mathematics (STEM) increasingly needed, it is no longer sufficient to teach science without including civic engagement as a major component. The ultimate goal of civic engagement and service learning in the sciences is not only to increase all students' scientific literacy, but also to empower students to be socially effective change agents, regardless of whether or not they pursue science as a career or even as a major. By blurring the distinctions between scientist, community member, teacher, and learner, citizen science can be a powerful content-delivery vehicle that aligns with emerging educational practices of active learning, hands-on inquiry, and the student-driven classroom. By taking science out of the classroom and into the park, onto the beach, or even into the town hall meeting, citizen science makes science relevant to students and to community members, reinforcing the concept that everyone can and should participate in science-based activities and activism as engaged members of their communities.

CITIZEN AS SCIENTIST

Historically, the terms *citizen* and *scientist* have not often appeared in a single phrase. Because of their specialized, technical training and the fact that their findings were generally distributed among "their own" in the form of peer-reviewed journals, scientists were often perceived by the general public as individuals who used mysterious methods to collect and analyze data, emerging periodically to share the insights they had gleaned, while citizens were passive recipients of expert knowledge. Scientists informed the citizenry like professors inform students or adults inform children. Yet the idea that science is an unassailable body of knowledge accumulated throughout history by professional scientists is long outmoded. Scientists are the first to admit that they do not have all the answers, and that what answers they do have are often flawed or incomplete. Nowhere is this more evident than within the natural sciences, where new species are discovered frequently while others go extinct before even being noticed.

With biodiversity declining and the pace of climate change increasing rapidly, ecologists are quickly seeing more and more connections between local species and global trends. The size, scope, and far-reaching implications of these connections necessitate long-term and geographically extensive studies. Such megastudies on wide-ranging or migratory species take decades to complete and require a virtual army of researchers collecting data in perfect synchrony over thousands of square miles. Citizen science has the potential to provide that army of researchers to address large-scale questions.

Some of the earliest examples of citizen science arose well before the term was coined, when large groups of people began monitoring large-scale events. Indeed, although citizen science is a relatively new term, the idea of nonscientists collecting valid scientific data has been around for a long time. Ordinary citizens have for centuries carefully monitored important ecological events such as the annual blooming of the cherry blossoms in Japan, a culturally significant occurrence anxiously awaited by all and carefully tracked by those in charge of planning associated festivities. In other geographic locations, other seasonal events—such as the ripening of grapes in vineyards, maturing of apples in orchards, and spawning of salmon in rivers—have been awaited and closely monitored generation after generation. The scientific study of such seasonal events is known as phenology. These events were once critical economic benchmarks. Before the era of refrigeration, factory farming, and the Walmart economy of instant access to resources 365 days a year, entire communities had to be ready to harvest, process, and store the season's crop, catch, or flock within as little as a week. A long and rich historical record carefully created by monks, farmers, and game wardens has allowed climate scientists and ecologists to piece together a timeline of seasonal events that is both relevant to and valuable in answering today's most pressing ecological questions.

> *Although citizen science is a relatively new term, the idea of nonscientists collecting valid scientific data has been around for a long time*

The patterns that have emerged from these records show some startling shifts in the timing and magnitude of phenological events. Some patterns have been tracked by amateur naturalists for decades through projects like the annual Audubon Christmas Bird Count, which began in 1900 and has allowed scientists to track bird species' responses to climate change. While birding often requires expensive equipment and the expertise needed to identify birds can take years to develop, other citizen science projects require minimal training and virtually no equipment. And while some birds can be difficult to spot and identify, many species that impact birds, such as raptors or felines, are easy to spot and identify, even for an inexperienced observer. Because citizen science does not require expert-level scientific skills, it offers a large variety of opportunities for the public to become involved in many different branches of scientific activity, ranging from identifying planets using satellite images to documenting the arrival of migratory butterflies or tracking the process of bud break and flower blooming in a schoolyard tree.

By involving the populace in aspects of environmental monitoring, citizen science can create meaningful civic engagement with the potential for cascading effects. Projects that focus on air or water quality can be especially effective in engaging participants in the scientific process at multiple stages, including question formulation, study design, data collection protocol development, data gathering and analysis, and presentation of results to government officials. Generally driven by grassroots interest in the effects of environmental changes on human health, such projects often represent collaborative efforts between community groups and educational institutions. They may originate when community groups become interested in studying a local environmental issue, leading them to contact an educational institution for scientific support and engage with the institution in investigating the issue. These investigations should be mutually beneficial, with the community group receiving support in developing a scientifically rigorous project and the educational institution gaining an opportunity to collect data on a large scale and engage students in applied research. One example of this model is the Alliance for Aquatic Resource Monitoring (ALLARM), based at Dickinson College in Pennsylvania, which has been working with community groups since 1986 to monitor local waterways while improving scientific literacy and creating advocates whose work benefits the broader community.

As humankind faces enormous environmental challenges and the hard choices that come with those challenges, it is crucial that citizens have the scientific literacy to evaluate information received through the media that is relevant to their lives and effectively advocate for change through the political process. By actively engaging the populace in scientific research, citizen science helps create a population that can achieve both ends. Since the data collected by participants in citizen science projects feed into large datasets that scientists will analyze, participants must collect those data in a uniform way to ensure quality. This need for quality data mandates that participants receive some training before participating in a citizen science project. Such training often occurs through interaction with the experiment's lead researcher, who can engage the participant on multiple levels—explaining not only the nature of the question being studied, but also how the researcher gathers data to address that question, what the participant's role is in the process, how the researcher will analyze and use the data, etc. This training is an important first step in empowering the participant as an active scientist and advocate. Every participant in a citizen science project has his or her own network of peers, family members, and colleagues. As participants share the information they gain from the project throughout these networks, they can produce profound ripple effects on knowledge that are impossible to quantify.

THE CHALLENGES OF TEACHING AND LEARNING SCIENCE

The practice of teaching and learning science presents a unique set of challenges and opportunities. Most science classes involve laboratory exercises, which typically entail prolonged experiments conducted by students who follow explicit, step-by-step directions under the close supervision of a lab instructor. In recent decades, so-called "cookbook chemistry," where each experiment has a single, predictable, and "correct" outcome, has been replaced—at least in theory—

by open-ended inquiry, where students apply theoretical concepts they learn in the classroom by designing and conducting unique experiments to test hypotheses they have developed. But students rarely achieve seamless execution of such hands-on inquiry in practice, in part because they lack practical experience collecting scientific data. Even when students do carry out well-designed and carefully executed experiments, they rarely believe that they have collected useful data or that their conclusions are valid. Citizen science can give students experience and increased confidence in their abilities to collect scientific data, as well as illustrating the importance of their efforts as their data contribute to a broader scientific context.

While many children have a natural curiosity and aptitude for science, at some point in their educations, students may be turned off to science and may even develop an aversion to the field. This aversion can be transmitted to children through parents, teachers, or other role models, who may even stigmatize students who excel in science and encourage them to focus on other disciplines. Past experiences of aversion and stigmatization can seriously diminish a college student's inclination to pursue a career in science or even take a science course, given the feelings of anxiety and stress students may experience at the very thought of such endeavors. Active learning outside of the classroom or in a lab setting—including through citizen science—can be a powerful means of combatting this anxiety, reigniting an interest in science, and replacing some negative associations with positive experiences and perhaps even a sense of empowerment.

Citizen science is also an effective way to help students quickly understand that ordinary citizens can collect valid scientific data, and that scientists frequently use data collected by community members for their own research. Students can quickly come to see that data collected by scientists is often indistinguishable from data collected by nonscientists, and that scientists frequently use historical observations made by laypeople who had not used scientific protocols. Ethnobotany is perhaps the most well-known scientific discipline where the traditional knowledge of shamans, midwives, priests, and farmers is painstakingly recorded by botanists. These trained scientists often spend years as apprentices to such healers, who likely never attended high school and have no formal scientific training whatsoever. In conjunction with the idea of citizen science, exposure to such nontraditional scientific realms can be an effective means of encouraging students to re-evaluate their notions about scientific research and expand their definitions of researcher, scientist, educator, and learner. Such exposure can also empower students to see that a lack of formal scientific training or prior knowledge is by no means a hindrance to conducting scientific research, and that they can in fact contribute meaningfully to the body of scientific knowledge. Citizen science can thus demystify the process of collecting data and empower students to call themselves scientists. Some citizen science research aims to monitor environmental trends and track vulnerable species on a scale large enough to allow scientists to see patterns that cannot be detected on a smaller scale. The opportunity to participate in protecting and building understanding of a vulnerable species can be particularly compelling for students. Students also become excited about a scientific topic if it is relevant to them and if it affects their community.

Not everyone wants to save the rainforest, particularly if they see that ecosystem as a theoretical abstraction. But when given the opportunity to roll up their sleeves and their pant legs and study their own neighborhoods, students become more connected to the subject matter and the species they encounter. This sense of connection and local relevance can serve as the first step toward activism and full civic engagement. Once students study something as common as a crab or a gull, they are far less likely to overlook that species in their daily lives.

Through formal and informal teaching experiences that help students acquire awareness as well as the skills and opportunity to make a difference, faculty can help students grow from disengaged and passive learners into informed activists and effective change agents who are connected with their communities. In this context, *activism* can be either political or apolitical but entails taking action to foster change; in the case study outlined below, for example, activism is volunteer-based scientific data collection used to monitor and protect local ecosystems. Similarly, *community* signals a broader ecological context that includes nonhuman populations with whom we humans interact and depend (e.g., plants, pollinators, and decomposers). Every observation made by each citizen scientist contributes tangibly to a large-scale scientific study with profound implications, and unlike traditional versions of "activism" where students lobby or protest for change, students engaged in citizen science are directly effecting change through their observations.

As the case study below indicates, once students have been directly involved in a scientific research project that is part of a bigger citizen science undertaking, they can show remarkable dedication to continued involvement, lasting far beyond the semester and even beyond graduation. Sometimes they even pass their commitment on to their children. At Kingsborough Community College (KCC), numerous students who have completed less than one season of field work have expressed a desire to continue working on a project, even when there are no funds or grades at stake. These students enjoy knowing that they are part of something special and important and feel that, through the research, they are enacting tangible change.

CITIZEN SCIENCE AND ACTIVISM AT A COMMUNITY COLLEGE:
A CASE STUDY

Although getting students out of the classroom may be challenging, doing so has immense benefits, not least of which is engaging students as active learners and activists. Located in the New York City Borough of Brooklyn, KCC students study in one of the most diverse cities in the world, and they approach learning with myriad experiences, expectations, and perspectives. Because the vast majority of these students have little experience in nature as a spectator, let alone as a researcher, a group project focused on nature can be a powerful means of unifying a diverse and otherwise often disjointed group of students. Conducting citizen science research in nature can bridge divides in experience, while capitalizing on the variety of experiences people bring. Getting everyone out in nature, where they have little experience, is one means to level the playing field.

One KCC project that has been particularly effective involves working with the New York City Audubon Society (NYC Audubon) to collect data on the

Atlantic horseshoe crab (*Limulus polyphemus*). While not as captivating on its surface as a rhinoceros or a polar bear, this ancient mariner—whose species is older than the dinosaurs—is remarkable in its own right. In fact, these armored, brown, overturned mixing bowls trundling through the surf may be the unsung superheroes of the invertebrate world. The crabs are valuable as bait and as food, and they play an indispensable role in the biomedical industry, which uses a protein in their blood to test for bacterial contamination on surgical instruments and implantable devices. Despite their unique lifesaving ability, their role as a critical food supply for migratory shorebirds is what interests NYC Audubon. Because their eggs provide a nutrient-rich source of fat and protein essential for endangered birds such as the red knot, which consumes the eggs before its annual hemispherical migration, NYC Audubon has incorporated activities to monitor and protect spawning horseshoe crabs into its larger program focused on understanding and mitigating threats to migratory shorebirds.

Every spring since 2009, teams of NYC Audubon volunteers greet the crabs as they arrive on the beaches of New York City's Jamaica Bay. Equipped with clipboards, quadrats (square-meter structures that circumscribe the plot to be sampled), and a modicum of training, these volunteers systematically count the crabs along the beach to gain an estimate of the total number found on that stretch of beach. Taking place in May and June around each new and full moon, the surveys last approximately two hours and occur at high tide, which coincides with the peak of spawning activity. Survey participants sometimes also tag crabs to track their movements. Since tags are deployed by volunteers and reported by beachgoers, this entire project depends on citizen scientists, some of whom do not even know they are participating in data collection until they dial the phone number on the tag.

In the spring of 2013, Professor Colon piloted a citizen science project approach involving students in this monitoring project. In order to train a cohort of students taking an elective Ecology class, Colon scheduled a one-hour citizen science training during the annual campus-wide Eco-Festival, which takes place in April to coincide with Earth Day. The timing was fortuitous, as it allowed the training to take place just before the spring horseshoe crab spawning season. The training was carried out by a veteran NYC Audubon citizen scientist volunteer coordinator and former student. This worldly yet down-to-earth woman was in some ways more effective than a polished professional would be in communicating with students due to her unwavering dedication to solving environmental problems through grassroots community action and her willingness to share her expertise and enthusiasm. While from a very different background from the students, the volunteer educator truly embodied civic engagement, which helped illuminate the point that environmental issues affect us all equally. The solutions to these problems are in each of our hands, provided we are willing to donate the time and energy required to enact change, promote awareness, and demonstrate civic engagement.

Once trained, students became official volunteers of NYC Audubon, which encouraged them to participate in at least one horseshoe crab survey on a local beach. Audubon's liability insurance covered the students, and Audubon assumed all risks associated with the field trips. Because Audubon's volunteer corps comprises a different demographic from the KCC student population, participating in Audubon's citizen science program gave students the opportunity to interact with members of entirely different segments of society, who instantly became their research peers and colleagues. On the beach, everyone gets wet, everyone has a job to do, and everyone works together as a team to serve the survival needs of an odd-looking invertebrate and an elusive species of bird they may not even be able to identify.

Many educators have observed that even the most resistant learner is invariably drawn to at least one of three things in nature: the disgusting, the adorable, or the helpless. Horseshoe crabs are apparently all three. Their seemingly mechanical appendages, daunting size, and alien-like appearance make them irresistible to even the most jaded student. Once assured that they are not dangerous, but in fact quite vulnerable, many students quickly muster the courage to touch or hold one. From there, it's a short progression to wanting to rescue those stranded by the high tide, which may perish in the hot sun while waiting for the next tide to arrive. In fact, once students have begun rescuing stranded crabs, it can be almost impossible to get them to stop—a phenomenon that was both frustrating and heartening to witness. It appears that the difference between overlooking and celebrating particular species truly lies in students' education.

With luck, a student will spot on the crab an unusual shell adornment: an identification tag. The instructor can use this discovery to introduce the topic of scientific research that uses mark-recapture techniques with crabs. Volunteers from NYC Audubon and numerous other environmental organizations deploy the tags by the thousands with the goal that some will be seen by beachgoers who will take the time to report their discovery, adding data to the United States Fish and Wildlife Service's database. The students are awed by the number of tags that must be deployed in order for a few crabs to be retrieved and reported. They quickly begin to see the magnitude of the research project and begin to understand the importance of their role in studying this seemingly irrelevant invertebrate.

During the training and the class trip, several students who had participated in research the previous summer readily agreed to help out. Such peer teaching further blurred the distinction between expert and learner. This two-way exchange not only benefited mentees, but also allowed mentors to gain valuable leadership skills by sharing their knowledge and experience with others. This benefit to the mentors first became evident during a presentation to the KCC administration, in which an otherwise shy research student was so eager to share her knowledge about the crabs that she commandeered the microphone to answer a question from the audience. On another occasion, a different student exhibited mentorship when he conducted a field trip to one of the Jamaica Bay crab monitoring sites with his daughter's middle school class to teach his daughter and her classmates about horseshoe crabs. Another student whose performance in the classroom had been unremarkable went on to win honors at a local conference for his outstanding field research. While these examples may have been exceptions to the rule, they illustrate seamless continua between KCC students' roles as learners and their roles as parents, educators, and citizens that can serve as models for the desired outcomes of civic engagement. And while not all students will emerge from a single citizen science experience similarly motivated to share their knowledge with the community, data show positive correlations between exposure to nature and a desire to experience, promote, and protect nature.[1]

All of the students' experiences on the beach corresponded with learning opportunities: collecting data in the form of observations and samples, interacting with their research peers and members of the general public, and seeing the amount of debris that washes up on the beach and how it affects every species in the ecosystem. The fact that many students had been affected by Superstorm Sandy made it all the more important and relevant to engage them in helping to promote beaches, ecosystems, and communities that are healthy for both humans and other species. A post-semester focus group approximately six weeks after the field trip and a week after the semester ended indicated that students sensed the relevance of the horseshoe crab training and research project. Students claimed to be more aware of local environmental issues and felt more obligated not to litter and to clean up their environment. They felt the information they were learning during the Ecology course became more real as a result of the field trip, and they reported being more aware of the ecosystems and species in their communities.

CONCLUSION

Kingsborough Community College's institutional commitment to civic engagement is evident in the implementation of a civic engagement requirement for all students. This requirement can be fulfilled in different ways (through volunteer work, coursework related to social issues, or even outside experiences). In providing students the opportunity to fulfill civic engagement through citizen science, the institution is not only acknowledging but also encouraging students' civic practice. In fact, when CUNY created the Jamaica Bay Institute for Science and Resilience to promote the restoration of urban ecosystems, it also created the ideal conditions for KCC to engage students in citizen science as a means of fulfilling their civic engagement requirements in a way that is locally relevant, ecologically significant, and community driven. In an era of rising sea levels and climate change, students who live and study in close proximity to the sea are not only the first to be affected by severe storms, but also the first to see the value of monitoring local wetland species. By engendering the ethic of community engagement in students and empowering them with the tools to enact change, KCC can serve as a model of how to achieve civic engagement through citizen science for college campuses around the country and around the globe.

NOTE

1. For examples of this positive correlation, see Louise Chawla, "Significant Life Experiences Revisited: A Review of Research on Sources of Environmental Sensitivity," *The Journal of Environmental Education* 29, no. 3 (1998): 11–21; and Elizabeth K. Nisbet and John M. Zelenski, "Underestimating Nearby Nature: Affective Forecasting Errors Obscure the Happy Path to Sustainability," *Psychological Science* 22, no. 9 (2011): 1101–06.

6 Civility, Social Media, and Higher Education: A Virtual Triangle

Sybril Bennett

CIVILITY, as defined by Yale University Law Professor, Stephen L. Carter, "is the sum of the many sacrifices we are called to make for the sake of living together."[1] These sacrifices include being receptive to other citizens' ideas, ideals, or positions in order to respectfully hear what they have to say. This does not mean condoning or agreeing with others' views; but it does mean listening to and acknowledging another person's opinion as well as respecting the individual right to share an opinion. Students, as citizens with rights and responsibilities, need to learn to enact these principles, not only as they engage in their physical communities (such as the classroom), but also as they engage in communities online. Students must learn to be informed "digital citizens"—defined for the purpose of this discussion as those with the access, knowledge, comprehension, and skills to act responsibly online while respecting the democratic process.

It is up to educators to help students, as digital citizens, understand the concept of civility and how it applies in the real and virtual worlds. In order to accomplish this, those invested in higher education should create or adopt a more universal definition of civility. It is important to keep in mind that the question of who participates in crafting this definition will be as important as the definition itself. Those who participate in a particular community dictate the policies, procedures, and protocols of that community. Traditionally, higher education faculty, researchers, and administrators have defined concepts like civility and social media; but in the digital age, the balance of power has been redistributed. As media industry professionals have learned, once-passive audience members have now become producers as well as consumers. Anyone with on-line access can contribute to the conversation. No one person or group owns knowledge; no single entity has the sole responsibility for interpreting ideology, paradigms, or epistemologies.

It is nonetheless higher education's role to provide students with the context to understand the technological shifts they are experiencing, and to prepare students for the changing democratic world in which they live. In doing so, educators need to consider key relationships—students' roles as digital citizens, and social media as platforms for virtual communities—within the context of civic learning and teaching. Faculty and administrators at colleges and universities need to ask: What is the future of civility, civic democracy, and civic participation, both on- and off-line, in the educational industrial complex?

SOCIAL MEDIA, CIVILITY, AND HIGHER EDUCATION

Social media—an umbrella concept that encompasses social networking and other online activities—is a pervasive and powerful channel for distributing digitized information. The majority of social media content is now accessed via mobile devices. As of January 2014, 90 percent of adults own a cell phone, 58 percent of adults own a smartphone, more than 30 percent own e-readers, and more than 40 percent own tablets.[2] This is a seismic shift in a very short period time. Other media have taken decades, if not more than a century, to gain such a sizeable audience share.

It is possible to interpret social media narrowly, as including only social networks like Facebook, Twitter, Instagram, and Vine. But this would be a mistake. In his book *The Thank You Economy*, author and entrepreneur Gary Vaynerchuk argues that social media is neither media nor a platform, but instead is "a massive cultural shift that has profoundly affected the way society uses the greatest platform ever invented, the Internet."[3] This interpretation sheds light on how educators can understand and approach social media. When students have a question, they no longer raise their hands in a classroom to ask it; instead, they Google it. If they have a complaint against a faculty member, they do not wait to express it in their end-of-semester evaluations; they post their uncensored comments on RateMyProfessor.com. They consult experts in real time through global portals like Twitter; they create talk shows and host conversations using tools like Google Hangouts, Skype, and SoundCloud. These practices should influence how educators comprehend and define social media, especially in connection with civility. As students achieve greater access, educators acquire greater responsibility for helping students become digital citizens by teaching the democratic principle of civility as well as the role of social media in society.

Social media has changed the rules of civic engagement

These factors lend urgency to the task of training digital citizens. Students need guidance on how to navigate the evolving digital frontier. They need to learn the rules of the Internet superhighway, to understand that just because they *can* post their thoughts online does not mean that they *should*. Students do not always understand that each and every piece of content they publish, whether publicly or privately, can and will be seen. They need to learn that they can choose to freely voice their opinions, but they must accept responsibility for their words. In some ways, this maxim has always been true; but in others, social media has changed the rules of civic engagement.

For example, the social news and entertainment website Reddit hosts communities known as "subreddits." A number of subreddits support racism, sexism, and even pedophilia—objectionable topics to many people—but Reddit content managers protect the free speech rights of community participants. In a well-publicized incident, the popular blog Gawker published the identity of a user who moderated subreddits devoted to sharing controversial content and posted suggestive images of underage girls and similar photos taken of women without their knowledge or consent. Though many users found what the Reddit user posted deplorable, some users rallied to his defense, feeling that such public identification threatened freedom of speech. After his identity was revealed, this individual eventually lost his job and received death threats. In an effort to educate and empower more responsible digital citizens, a faculty member could easily use real-life and real-time events like this Reddit example to demonstrate the role of civility in online communities.

To offer an example related to off-line social networks, "one in six of the nation's 400 top colleges and universities currently have 'free speech zones.'"[4] But, in many cases, the policies used to govern the zones are unconstitutional, as they require students to gain permission and observe a waiting period before distributing literature. These zones also may be confined to a small area on campus. Like the Reddit example, the existence of these free speech zones offers a critical opportunity to help students reflect on their own actions as citizens, including how they promote and respect civility in social networks. The zones suggest one way that students can challenge offensive content in a civil manner; they also suggest the need for colleges to truly honor the First Amendment in practice and in policy. The existence of the zones is a sign that the transparency of the digital age might offer greater freedom of expression, but it also demands greater respect for individual and collective rights and responsibilities.

DIGITIZING CURRICULA: AN EDUCATOR'S GUIDE

In fall 2013, I created a pilot Digital Citizenship course at Belmont University in Nashville, Tennessee. The course focused on the nine elements of digital citizenship as described on the website digitalcitizenship.net: digital commerce, digital health and wellness, digital security, digital literacy, digital access, digital communication, digital etiquette, digital rights and responsibilities, and digital law.[5] In designing the course, I aimed to help students achieve learning outcomes like personal and social responsibility, including local and global civic knowledge and engagement.[6] I also aimed to help students develop digital skills, an area where US adults are behind globally. In a recent study comparing the math, literacy, and computer skills of US adults with those of adults in other nations under democratic rule, the United States ranked behind fourteen other countries.[7] Given the dire need for science, technology, engineering, and math majors, this research (and common sense) suggests that teaching digital skills is not an option, it is an imperative.

I designed the Digital Citizenship course to address the global need for digital citizens. I wanted it to prepare students to embrace their civic duty to contribute to the virtual world in responsible ways. The course would help students build digital skills and learn how to conduct themselves in a civil manner as professionals in virtual spaces. Students who completed the course would not only gain a better understanding of how to use social media tools—including Google, Twitter, and emerging social networks—but also would:

- develop a better understanding of their civic and ethical responsibilities in the digital realm;
- construct a current events snapshot of digital media;

- develop their critical and lateral thinking skills, as well as their ability to engage in "just-in-time learning";
- become active learners who are able to analyze, compare and contrast, and apply acquired knowledge;
- enhance their presentation skills, both on- and off-line; and
- improve their collaborative problem-solving skills.

In order to help students achieve these outcomes, I assigned group projects where students could build and strengthen their collaboration and presentation skills. I also created an online learning community to provide a guided experience for students as they practiced making substantive comments and contributions on the Web. Social platforms like Google+, which combines Twitter-like updates with "social circles" to create functionality similar to that of Facebook's newsfeed, can be used to create private learning communities for students. Private communities, where participation is limited to those who are invited to join, are ideal when helping students build confidence in their ability to make substantive comments and critically analyze their own and their classmates' posts. In these environments, students can more freely express their ideas and share their voices. The opportunity to post, comment, and contribute to the online conversation while using their critical, comparative, and contextual learning skills helps to improve student learning outcomes substantially.

By helping students understand the balance between empirical and emotive language, showing them the elements of democratic discourse, and encouraging them to embrace their curiosity, conscience, and critical thinking skills, faculty members can make a significant contribution toward civility. Each assignment in the Digital Citizenship course was tailored toward this end. Students received individual grades for their participation in the online Google+ community, as well as for their in-class participation and class attendance. They also received a shared grade for their group work, which included analyzing new media giants (including Twitter, Amazon, LinkedIn, Google, and Facebook) and proposing a mobile app idea connected to the latest technology in wearable computers. To provide support for their revenue and marketing plans, students conducted extensive research on their target audience and expected competition.

Current events and technologies provided examples of how to apply critical thinking to digital content and offered opportunities to encourage digital citizenship. For example, students studied the case of Edward Snowden, a former employee of the Central Intelligence Agency and a former contractor for the National Security Agency who released hundreds of thousands of pages of classified documents to select members of the press. These documents showed that sections of the US government were collecting extensive information, including data on cell phone usage and web activity, on foreign and domestic populations without the knowledge of US citizens. Government officials defended these actions as protecting US citizens; Snowden said he was concerned about the privacy of those citizens. Whether his actions were right or wrong, Snowden sought asylum in Russia as the United States explored ways to extradite him. This case study provided a real-world example of the informed decisions digital citizens must make. Students discussed their thoughts about Snowden's actions in class, and they shared articles, made comments, and posted videos in the Google+ community. When engaging in these activities, students were encouraged to go beyond their feelings to embrace the facts.

As they analyzed the Snowden case, students learned that respect should be an inseparable part of digital citizenship. Some students called Snowden a traitor, while others thought he was a hero—reflecting the division of the larger public's views. But regardless of their personal opinions, students were able to have an engaged, honest, and truly democratic conversation, supported by appropriate prompts and a series of videos and articles shared on- and off-line that promoted informed discussion.

Additionally, students learned that adaptability and flexibility are not optional in the digital age. To demonstrate this lesson, each class activity built upon previously acquired skills and demonstrated the value of "just-in-time learning"—where students learn a needed skill just in time to use it. In the course, students learned how to use new presentation platforms to create "Prezi," an interactive presentation software that communicates information beyond that which is possible to convey with PowerPoint. They also learned to work together and honor each other's strengths, further contributing to their understanding of the notion of citizenship.

Another classroom activity designed to educate digital citizens who respect each other's rights, responsibilities, and research involved a project focused on Google Glass, a commercially available wearable computer like something one might see in *Star Trek*. This wearable technologic device allows the user to experience hands-free augmented reality. Information such as directions, weather forecasts, and email messages seem to appear in the atmosphere in front of the user. The device will even read data aloud.

As a final course project, students created mobile apps for Google Glass. One group created an app to help users navigate while jogging; another group created an app that would help keep nature lovers safe by mapping surrounding terrain, identifying plants and birds, and providing information about weather conditions. The project provided students with an engaging, interactive experience in which they embraced a digital tool that citizens will encounter. We also discussed the privacy, security, ethical, and legal issues surrounding Google Glass. The students benefited greatly from the hands-on experience of working with this technology and applying it to real-life situations.

Wearable computer technology like Google Glass directly affects the role and reality of digital citizens. The speed and innovation of technology, as well as social media specifically, are changing how users interact with each other and the world. As the boundaries of ethics, privacy, and security continue to stretch, educators must prepare students to think critically and to act with civility. To achieve this goal, courses like Digital Citizenship should be a mandatory part of the collegiate experience.

Finally, qualitative data captured from student comments can serve as a potential source for undergraduate research. In the Google+ community, students shared data as events took place. This community commentary provided a snapshot of what was happening in the digital environment in real time and created an initial database for collaborative undergraduate research, as well as for course evaluation. Asking students specific questions about what they knew prior to taking the course, what they learned during the course and what assignments were the most educational will allow for further research. Due to the amount and availability of digital data, students said that taking the course was like drinking from a fire hose. Each and every day there was a new and seemingly more pressing issue in the news, from surveillance and security to the digital divide and beyond. By addressing these issues in the classroom, students learned technological terms, tackled topics pertaining to surveillance, and even created mobile applications from Google Glass.

In the final class session, we revisited the notion of digital citizenship. I asked students working in small groups to define "digital citizen." Each group posted a draft definition on Twitter and shared it with the class. I recorded their ideas on the board and then made a list of the terms they had in common. Next, we identified the common words and themes. Using this shortened list, students worked in their groups to craft a revised definition for "digital citizen." Here are two examples of the definitions posted the second time:

- "A citizen who is involved in and informed about issues that pertain to the digital world, and are [sic] willing to adapt to ever-changing new technologies."
- "An informed individual who can efficiently adapt to the digital world in a professional and responsible manner."

CONCLUSION

In order to be a true digital citizen, one must embrace civility and social media. The Web has become a platform for collaborating, connecting, sharing, and creating community locally, nationally, and globally. Every community has rules. As participants join, they must adhere to ethical tenets and possess a sense of civility. Teaching digital citizens means returning higher education to its philosophical roots: the higher ground upon which most academic institutions were founded. In the twenty-first century, that higher ground is a basis for promoting the public good by preparing well-informed users for social media spaces and the digital experiences.

I often say that online, your sins may be forgiven, but they will not be forgotten. In the digital age, authenticity, transparency, and data will be public and permanent for eternity. The ability of faculty to analyze content, provide context, and critique data remains invaluable. However, the realm in which these skills are applied has now shifted from the classroom alone to the latest distribution platforms. The magnitude of technological adoption requires faculty to pause and to change. Just as most professors have finally let go of the overhead projector, faculty must also abandon some older notions of teaching as a one-directional experience like television or radio. Leading the voyage into the digital wilderness is imperative. Go afraid—just go.

In this climate, the ultimate act of incivility is to ignore, dismiss, and demonize the digital landscape. The digital world is the world into which students will graduate. It is our world, and no amount of apathy is going to end the digital revolution. Students' participation isn't optional, and neither is anyone else's. Content and wisdom should be leveraged on- and off-line. As digital citizens, we need to learn all we can about this frenetic and frightening, yet exhilarating, new world. To do any less would be uncivil and irresponsible. Students must be educated and empowered to become digital citizens, and it is higher education's duty to prepare them. Faculty owe students, as fellow passengers in this virtual world, learning experiences that promote democratic discussion, civility, and empathy for others. Social media, the latest distribution tool with the greatest international reach, just makes the necessity more pressing. Indeed, for faculty, administrators, and students who are behaving as informed and educated digital citizens, civility—"the sum of the many sacrifices"—is the act of learning how to respect each other's culture, roots, and realities in a digital world.

NOTES

1. Stephen L. Carter, *Civility* (New York: Basic Books, 1998), 11.
2. Pew Research Internet Project, "Mobile Technology Fact Sheet," (Washington, DC: Pew Research Center, 2014), http://www.pewinternet.org/fact-sheets/mobile-technology-fact-sheet.
3. Gary Vaynerchuk, *The Thank You Economy* (New York: Harper Collins, 2011), 5.
4. Charles Haynes discusses the problematic implications of free speech zones in "Free speech is being zoned out on campus," Foundation for Individual Rights in Education (blog), October 4, 2013, http://www.thefire.org/free-speech-is-being-zoned-out-on-campus.
5. Mike Ribble, "Nine Themes of Digital Citizenship," *Digital Citizenship*, accessed August 22, 2014, http://digitalcitizenship.net/Nine_Elements.html.
6. These outcomes correspond to the Essential Learning Outcomes detailed in the Association of American Colleges and Universities' Liberal Education and America's Promise (LEAP) campaign. See "Liberal Education and America's Promise (LEAP)," Association of American Colleges and Universities, accessed December 17, 2013, http://www.aacu.org/leap.
7. D. D. Guttenplan, "O.E.C.D. Warns West on Education Gaps," *New York Times*, December 8, 2013, http://www.nytimes.com/2013/12/09/world/asia/oecd-warns-west-on-education-gaps.html.

Retooling the University: Critical Thinking, Creative Play, Collaboration and Participatory Public Art

7

Carole Frances Lung

UNIVERSITIES ARE CURRENTLY A DYSFUNCTIONAL COMBINATION of impossible bureaucratic policies and highly conventional institutional practices. But they can mend this dysfunction by prioritizing the arts, engaged learning, service learning, and civic learning. To achieve this prioritization, the higher education community needs to re-envision the university by building an infrastructure that provides the means for students to acquire interdisciplinary knowledge and create new ways of knowing within various community contexts. Institutions that are able to commit resources (financial, intellectual, social, etc.) to developing this infrastructure will be preparing students for a more stable future, wherein they will have the skills to imagine and obtain their goals by assessing risk, being willing to fail, and reflecting on the process of personal growth.

Publicly funded universities are struggling to find their place at a time when for-profit education is expanding, capital and interactions are circulating rapidly in virtual worlds, and hedge funds and startups with fast turn overs and big profit margins are replacing other resources as the main driver of economic growth and social mobility. Because of this, today's students need to observe, shadow, and perhaps intern with professionals in order to understand how to adapt their particular field of study to a real-world setting. To make the best of their college experiences, students also need to reflect on their goals, make informed decisions, and understand why they are attending college in the first place. When students understand how a higher education will affect their life, and are prepared to engage with the institution and use education as a tool to achieve their goals, they will be better served by the faculty and administration.

The ultimate aim of the university should be to nurture the creation of whole persons. As part of this goal, we need to educate students to be citizens who recognize that they do not exist in isolation—a goal that requires every university across the country to consciously and cooperatively retool itself as a site for collaboration, experimentation, and experiential learning. Faculty in all disciplines must recognize and grasp the composite character of the university both as a holistic entity (consisting of a shared geography, the student body, the faculty, the staff, and the administration) and as a place that fosters expertise in different domains. The university's value lies in the complex relationships it can foster between those who hold various forms of knowledge and the internal and external communities, both local and global, of which it is a part. To realize this value, however, institutions must first recognize the utility of facilitating these relationships. In particular, the university should seek to improve the ability of students to participate in creating knowledge within these various community contexts.

Retooling universities for the twenty-first century means turning institutions into places where rigorous learning occurs in supportive environments. The old model of learning, in which students focused on following directions, meeting deadlines, and memorizing facts, is not the model of the future. In the twenty-first century, the learning environment must allow students to explore and experiment on their own terms, with the support and guidance of the faculty. In the retooled model of higher education, faculty and students work as co-researchers who explore the world together. The retooled model emphasizes smaller classrooms over large-scale efficiency. It fosters engaged learning by bringing the local community onto the campus and into the classroom—and by taking the classroom to the streets. This model provides students with opportunities to meet people of different ages and demographics, diversifying the campus by allowing students to meet and learn from people from all walks of life.

THE AIMS OF RETOOLING THE UNIVERSITY

The future of the university depends on retooling to make art—and with it, creative problem solving—the center of university education. In the retooled university, interdisciplinary art and collaboration can provide needed personal interactions drawing on a range of implicit and peripheral forms of communication, creative brainstorming techniques, consensus-building and decision-making activities, and collaborative projects. The retooled university is a unique place to explore, analyze, and strengthen connections between social activism and artistic practice.

In this vision of retooling, the university as a whole must declare that "everyone is an artist"

In this vision of retooling, the university as a whole must declare that "*everyone* is an artist." When Joseph Beuys, a politically engaged activist German artist, originally asserted this approach, he did not necessarily believe that every person would be a practicing artist. Rather, he believed that each person—whether a doctor, lawyer, educator, homemaker, or musician—should attempt to infuse creative thinking and action into his or her life practice. Embracing this expansive idea of who artists are and what art is would broaden and blur the conventional definition of "art." "Social sculpture"—"a conscious act of shaping, of bringing some aspect of the environment…from a chaotic state into a state of form"—would be at the core of our existence. Art would shape politics, economics, education, and environment. Life would be created like art—critically, conceptually, and collectively. "All around us," he said, "the fundamentals of life are crying out to be shaped, or created."[1]

ESSENTIAL FOUNDATIONS OF THE RETOOLED UNIVERSITY

So what will the retooled university look like when it has adapted to this changing environment? I suggest that it will not "look" so much as "be." The university of the future will be virtual, participatory, and collaborative, with multidisciplinary engagement between community, students, faculty, and staff. Social networking, online student groups, student-run websites, student- and community-run co-ops, socially engaged businesses, and off-campus learning sites are just some of the practices it will support. I offer the following vision of the structural components—the core principles and terms—that will compose the retooled university.

Core Principles
- Art and activism are interchangeable.
- Art can transform civic learning into a dynamic and playful visual experience that draws people in.
- An aesthetic eye and a creative hand are essential for building a better world.
- Everyone has an artistic life that they can use to transform their personal activism.
- Cultural transformation is necessary for lasting change.
- Civic learning is a pathway to creative engagement.

Core Terms
1. Critical Thinking
2. Reflection
3. Creative Play
4. Interdisciplinary Curriculum
5. Socially Engaged Practice
6. Collaboration

Critical Thinking

Critical thinking is essential for generating participatory public art experiences and exploring meaning. Moreover, the creative atmosphere such art engenders further encourages students, faculty, and community members to consciously consider participating in their own society. Being self-reflective, reflective of situations around you, and an articulate speaker is at the core of critical thinking.

The retooled university would encourage activist projects like the Yes Men, which couples critical thinking with humor and thrift-store suits. Performers Jacques Service and Igor Vamos attempt to unravel corporate greed by posing as top corporate executives at business conferences. Through websites, films, and other forms of media, they parody and critique corporate targets in extreme ways, attempting to awaken their audiences to the dangers of corporate practices. Operating under the premise that lies can expose the truth, the Yes Men practice what they call "Identity Correction."[2]

The tools for critical thinking can be developed in the classroom through the processes of critique. Critiques are a challenging and safe opportunity for students to present work and to review the work of their peers. In this process, student artists present their work, and their peers offer verbal and written responses focused on how the work communicates the artist's intent. This exercise helps students explore how a particular piece is communicating, functioning, engaging, or failing. Students evaluate and consider the context of how the object, performance, interaction, project, or event, is being used and perceived by the public audience—building valuable critical thinking skills along the way.

Reflection
The processes of critical thinking and critique highlight another essential element of the retooled university: student-directed reflection. Students should review their own and each other's work frequently. This practice encourages knowledge transfer from student to student, thus allowing works to develop and evolve. As students develop an expanded vocabulary of engagement through peer interaction, they are able to discuss the processes of their learning in ways that help to de-personalize the critique itself and enable individual students to help each other grow. By engaging in critiques, students learn to implement vocabulary, analyze what they are experiencing, and speak publicly.

In the critique process, failure also is an opportunity for reflection. In the retooled university, by replacing "the test" with processes like presentations and critiques, we teach students to embody their educational experiences and to embrace successes and failures. The key is for students to develop the skills of observation and awareness, and to learn from the processes of making, presenting, speaking, listening, and participating. According to the Center for Critical Thinking, "Such thinking entails the intellectually disciplined process of actively and skillfully conceptualizing, applying, analyzing, synthesizing, and evaluating information gathered from or generated through observation, experience, reflection, reasoning, or communication, and involves deriving from that process a guide to belief and action."[3]

Creative Play
The retooled university should also enlist creative play as a methodology for developing practical social skills. Creative play in art encourages participation as a social activity and promotes group cohesion. Through the collective participation in art, both the spectator and the artist are engaged. Creative play is the charge that flows through the lines of communication; it forms an essential connection between the artist and the audience. Through creative play, participants (audience members) develop the agency that comes with attaining self-knowledge and establishing meaning in everyday experience. As beings in the world, we are always seeking immediacy as we try to connect with our surroundings and our-selves. Thus, we are always negotiating and confronting our lives. Creative play is a method through which we can decipher those meanings through interaction.

In 2010, as an Exceptional Resident Artist at the Elsewhere Collaborative, I witnessed the exuberant energy and magical transformation that occur during creative play.[4] At the collaborative, resident artists spend two weeks to three months engaging with the materials found in the double store front, creating interactive installations, performances, and community events. While I was a resident, an event called "City" was held on the first Friday of the month.

"City" consisted of the artist and community participants becoming various city workers—bankers, bakers, school teachers, shop owners, mayors—and performing the roles and tasks of the various occupations. The event was an opportunity for visitors from all walks of life in Greensboro, NC to playfully engage in American norms and culture and to openly engage in varied perspectives and possibilities. "City" is an opportunity for intergenerational and intercultural play. Over time, Elsewhere's programs have evolved and the creative play opportunities offered have expanded to include a series of "Playshop" events, such as "Cooking Show," "Public Mending," and "Grandma Museum."[5]

It could be said that creative play just looks like what takes place in a kindergarten classroom. However, the activities are actually a challenge to the fast-paced, competitive world in which we all live, where we do not have time to play unless under the guise of networking. Creative play provides an opportunity to return to childhood and find meaning in the simple task of being.

Interdisciplinary Curriculum

The retooled university must also fully immerse faculty and students in interdisciplinary approaches. While the term "interdisciplinary" can be used to describe studies that draw on the methodology and insights of several established disciplines, "interdisciplinary" can also signify creating something new by thinking across disciplinary boundaries to foster multilayered ideas, projects, and experiences that can only occur when two or more disciplines come together.

One example of interdisciplinary campus partnerships is the work Dr. Samuel Landsberger and I have done with master's degree students in the Department of Mechanical Engineering and Kinesiology at California State University, Los Angeles. As an artist, I find that it is not always possible to generate objects that have function beyond their role as art. My work involves participatory sewing performances, through which I create social bonds and shared social spaces, emphasizing skills sharing and hands-on craft instruction that provide an alternative to the global garment industry. For this work, I wanted to develop a collaborative bicycle-powered sewing machine that I could use for performances or interventions on the streets of Los Angeles. This concept requires one person to contribute sewing skills and the other to provide power by pedaling the bike. My goals as an artist suggested the constraint that the machine should be mechanical (requiring a person to pedal it), not electrical. I took my idea to Dr. Landsberger and his students and asked them to create a useable design within the constraints of my goals. This provided the *students* with a more complicated challenge than that of simply designing and building a bike and required them to learn about aesthetics and how visual presentation affects audience experience. At the same time, the collaboration required *me* to reconsider the functional aspect of my work. Through this experiment, Dr. Landsberger and I facilitated active exchange in a hands-on environment, which contributed to both the students' and our learning and development.

By replacing "the test" with processes like presentations and critiques, we teach students to embrace successes and failures

Socially Engaged Practice

Additionally, retooled universities must implement socially engaged art practices. Existing in one form or another since the 1960s, socially engaged art movements arise in response to the sheer gluttony and decadence of the commercial art world and society in general. Socially engaged art explores the idea of imbuing art with meaning beyond its role as an object and commodity.

The feminist art movement of the late 1970s and early 1980s exemplified the concept of socially engaged art. For example, in *Three Weeks in May* (a series

of performances and events held during a three-week period in May 1977), artists like Suzanne Lacy and Leslie Labowitz, whose careers continue to address social issues today, exposed the extent of reported rapes in Los Angeles, raising national attention to the issue of violence against women.

In my own work, I have developed socially engaged practice through careful listening and skills sharing, organizing, and community building among students and community members through action and conversation. In 2006, I began my first socially engaged work, the Sewing Rebellion. Conceived while I was in graduate school, this work has helped to proliferate the motto "Stop Shopping, Start Sewing" across the United States and in Europe. The Sewing Rebellion continues to this day and has now inspired the next generation of Faux Fraus (trained Sewing Rebellion volunteers) who are facilitating, listening, and engaging in providing free sew-

"Frau Fiber traversing the streets of Los Angeles (above) and engaging with Los Angeles Participant (top), during the performance KO Enterprises: the American Brand.

ing skills to the public, in ways that exceed what I could do as a single artist. The Sewing Rebellion is one of a vast array of initiatives hatched by professional artists, nonprofit arts organizations, and social services organizations that are working to build community and social responsibility, and to provide meaning to our everyday experiences.[6]

Collaboration

The curriculum within the retooled university should emphasize collaborative initiatives within the institution and its surrounding local communities. Collaboration in art allows participants to set their egos aside for the sake of working toward a common idea. Collaboration is a powerful experience in which each voice can be heard and respected and participants can inform each other of how to improve the direction of the effort. The exchange of ideas and processes creates an atmosphere for experimentation that can often lead to outcomes that one would not have reached on his or her own. In collaborative art, all participants understand that the work is a mutual effort and that hierarchy is an impediment to final outcomes.

Open Space Technology represents one such form of creative collaboration. "In Open Space meetings, events and organizations, participants create and manage their own agenda of parallel working sessions around a central theme of strategic importance, such as: What is the strategy, group, organization or community that all stakeholders can support and work together to create?"[7] These collective spaces provide opportunities for people with diverse interests to come together to envision and enact innovative ideas.

Complaints Choirs are another example of a collaborative community whose members create a social sculpture art project. As participants in a Complaints Choir, community members sing their complaints about the cities in which they live. This work was conceived by artists Tellervo Kalleinen and Oliver Kochta-Kalleinen, who have directed choirs in Finland, Germany, Norway, Hungary, the United States, Canada, Australia, Israel, Singapore, Hong Kong, and the Netherlands. In Birmingham, UK, the government implemented changes in the bicycling and bus schedules in response to the complaints aired by the choir. Complaints Choirs' civic participation and emphasis on collaboration have helped to facilitate lasting changes in their respective cities.

CONCLUSION

With economies, governments, and urban and rural landscapes everywhere in need of change, the need to retool the university is urgent. When the mission, aims, principles, and terms of the retooled university have been implemented, the university will be a place where, as Bueys asserted, *everyone* truly is an artist. Our students will be prepared to address the local, national, and global issues of the twenty-first century; they will be able to apply critical and creative thinking and dialogues to any area of specialization. The retooled university will transform our current institutional cultures from static, congested, mired systems into fluid systems of cooperation, collaboration, and participation.

NOTES
1. Walker Art Center, "Creativity" (Minneapolis: Walker Art Center, 2014), http://www.walkerart .org/archive/8/9C430DB110DED6686167.htm.
2. The Yes Men project defines "Identity Correction" as "[i]mpersonating big-time criminals in order to publicly humiliate them, and otherwise giving journalists excuses to cover important issues." Accessed August 15, 2014, http://www.theyesmen.org.
3. The Critical Thinking Community, "Defining Critical Thinking" (Tomales, CA: The Foundation for Critical Thinking, 2013), http://www.criticalthinking.org/pages/defining-critical-thinking/766.
4. The Elsewhere Collaborative, founded by George Scheer and Stephanie Sherman in 2003, is a former thrift store located in Greensboro, North Carolina, that appears to be more like a museum than an art venue. The thrift store—a hoarder's wonderland—was owned and operated by Scheer's grandmother and has now been transformed and organized into a living museum. For more information, see http://www.goelsewhere.org/living-museum.
5. For more information about Playshops, visit http://www.goelsewhere.org/category/playshops.
6. Machine Project and KCHUNG Radio are also model socially engaged art initiatives. Machine Project is "a storefront space in the Echo Park neighborhood of Los Angeles that hosts events

about all kinds of things," including "scientific talks, poetry readings, musical performances, competitions, group naps, cheese tastings and so forth." Machine Project, "About Us" (Los Angeles: Machine Project, 2014), http://machineproject.com/about. KCHUNG is a volunteer-run pirate radio station that provides a platform for broadcasting music, news, and discussion to anyone who completes the one-hour training session. For more information on KCHUNG, visit http://news.kchungradio.org.

7. Michael Herman, "What Is Open Space Technology?" *Open Space World* (Chicago: Michael Herman Associates, 1998), http://www.openspaceworld.org/cgi/wiki.cgi?AboutOpenSpace.

Reflections on the Center of the Civic

Timothy K. Eatman

Introduction

The term *civic*, commonly used in reference to community-wide systems and processes, stems etymologically from the Latin *civicus* and is grounded in notions of deep human connectedness—indeed, of life and death. It harkens back to the fifteenth century, when a circular wreath or garland of oak leaves (*corona civica*) was awarded to one who saved the life of a fellow citizen in battle. This powerful symbol of care and protection affirms the best of what it means to live together in community, to be in fellowship, to advance a collective ethos in order to sustain shared values and goals that support health and growth in a society. At the *center of the civic*, one might argue, is the ability to truly see and respond to the urgent needs of others. And yet, in its prevailing contemporary connotation, engaging with "the civic" suggests engaging issues, processes, and texts in ways that tend to supplant these visceral, organic, community-grounded realities and dynamics. This is to say, for example, that while voter turnout, campaign volunteerism, and even legislative work are important expressions of civic engagement, it is a mistake for them to be seen as the most meaningful measures of civic life. The civic gestalt manifests most powerfully on the ground, in diverse relationships and through intentionally attending to often difficult to measure dynamics. The dominant prevailing ideologies about individualism and social status in our pluralistic, increasingly ahistorical society add to the challenge. Revisiting the etymology of the civic may prove a useful prompt toward raising our collective consciousness about the concept's community-engaged aspects.

The insightful chapters included in this volume prepare us to reflect on the center of the civic, which I believe is essential to effective and meaningful civic learning and teaching. Even as we consider innovative program models, refined pedagogical strategies, and increasingly sophisticated methods for enhancing civic consciousness at all levels throughout academe, it behooves us to also consider the grounding issue of true human connectedness. As scholars, we do well to celebrate the privileged spaces that the academy affords for systematic inquiry and critical analysis—while at the same time remaining cognizant of our unfortunate and pervasive penchant for hyperanalysis, which can easily (and so often does) eclipse what many of us believe to be the fundamental purpose of our work: real impact and amelioration.

To be sure, the myriad pressing public issues of our time require that the continuum of scholarship include the full range of knowledge-making practices, artifacts, and methodologies, from the traditional to the community-engaged. But what does this mean for our work in the academy as it concerns civic learning and teaching? What battles are we fighting? What wreaths do we earn? What do we find at the center of civic learning and teaching?

CREATING SPACES

I often describe the work of Imagining America: Artists and Scholars in Public Life (IA)—a national consortium of more than one hundred colleges and universities focusing on the academy's civic purposes with special emphasis on the humanities, art, and design fields—as "creating spaces where hearts and spirits meet minds for deep, impactful, sustained knowledge-making and healing."[1] I realize that words like "heart," "spirit," and "healing" may immediately turn off many academics, but I say them anyway as one small way of celebrating humanity and wholeness within the academy. Indeed, I evoke these "soft and fuzzy" terms here in the spirit of provocation that undergirds this monograph series. The philosophies and practices associated with civic learning and teaching are channels for refocusing and negotiating the balance between work that is intellectually interesting and work that is critically impactful. Of course, the nexus of the two types of work is often not very difficult to locate.

Many in the academy share my fear that—in spite of all our carefully constructed and rigorous study designs, data collection methods, analytical approaches, and assessments—we fail to see and understand the people implicated in our work. These overlooked people include community-based partners, students from diverse and traditionally underrepresented backgrounds, families struggling to meet the increasing costs of higher education, and contingent faculty members. But they also include faculty members on the shrinking tenure track, mid- and senior-level administrators, and trustees who often become caught up in the hellish status hierarchy and difficult politics of resource allocation that they face at almost every turn.

The most useful and constructive civic learning and teaching practices may help us create the kinds of spaces the academy needs to trigger and retrigger perpetual renewal of our consciousness about the need to really see each other and respond to each other's needs. In a recent *Chronicle of Higher Education* article, William Deresiewicz astutely points to the mechanical rhythms of our educational systems. He writes that we view

> … education as an engineering problem, the movement of information from one brain to another—not the development of intellectual capacities, not the ability to formulate questions or devise solutions to unfamiliar problems, not imagination and creativity, not the power to continue learning after college on your own (all of which are necessary, as any employer will tell you, for a successful career in the "information economy"), and certainly not personal growth or the discovery of meaning, let alone any kind of larger social purpose.[2]

To be clear, the field of civic learning and teaching holds great promise for improved student success and transformed cultural contexts, both on and off campus. However, in the hands of those who simply endeavor to apply these tools and approaches to normative purposes, these practices become limited or even duplicitous. Perhaps there are ways to evoke the notion of the center of the civic as a meme within the culture of academe.

COURAGEOUS PRACTICES

This volume's authors present several substantive and compelling examples of civic learning and teaching models that have the potential to be truly ameliorative. These models are innovative, well planned, built on strong evidentiary bases, and grounded in the compelling research—for example, the research on high-impact practices for student success.[3] From my vantage point as faculty co-director of Imagining America, I have the privilege of seeing an impressive range of similar examples. The examples that I view as both located at the center of the civic and representing the leading edge of civic learning and teaching reflect at least one of seven factors that are often seen as provocative or risky within the academy's dominant culture. Whether they are students, faculty, or community members, the stakeholders driving these models have the courage to

1. embed civic teaching and learning practices in the core curriculum;
2. promote multiple pathways for stimulating "civic professionalism"[4] across disciplines;
3. connect values and practices to meaningful institutional policies (e.g., faculty rewards);
4. encourage the development of connective tissue between academic and student affairs;
5. forge and sustain an integrated focus on diversity and inclusion in the context of rich interdisciplinary connections;
6. keep in view the economic impact and potential of civically engaged work;
7. model reciprocity in community–campus partnerships.

While fully unpacking these "courages" is beyond the scope of this afterword, I point here to several examples of innovative civic learning and teaching models that I believe also attend to the center of the civic.

The D.R.E.A.M. Freedom Revival

In the spirit of Imagining America's signature approach to foregrounding the cultural disciplines (humanities, arts, and design fields), I first point to a project sponsored by IA headquartered at Syracuse University. Founded by Kevin Bott, associate director of IA, the DREAM Freedom Revival (DFR) of Syracuse and Greater Central New York is a community-embedded participatory theater project that synergizes multiple aspects of the Syracuse community by promoting civic agency through the arts. Dr. Bott leads participants in this multidimensional project, a partnership with citizens and organizations throughout the community, to co-create musical theater productions with original music and comedic sketches focused on local issues of shared concern (e.g., educational inequity, women's reproductive rights, the civic standing of the elderly, corporate personhood). Drawing on Syracuse's long legacy of freedom movements and the region's history of evangelical tent revivals,[5] the company refers to its work as "a tent revival for freedom and democracy."[6] It combines the energy and communal spirit of religious revivals with the aesthetics and playfulness of musical comedy to point toward democratic renewal and to forge a powerful sense of celebratory, agentic community.[7] DFR participants include a wide range of Syracuse citizens including long time residents, seniors, college students, grandmothers, young professionals, and faculty. Performing in multiple venues around the city, the DFR invites audience members to participate by offering "testimony" (i.e., personal stories) about their relationships to the issue at hand. Now entering its fourth season, DFR will begin working with its partners to co-develop metrics for assessing community impact.

DFR connects the theory and history of nineteenth-, twentieth-, and twenty-first-century participatory and political theater to the practice of co-creating performance models in partnership with community partners. The project has led to the development of a course through drama or communication and rhetorical studies through which students wrestle with the same questions about the relationship between form and function and about the ethics of partnership that artists have considered since at least the early twentieth century. Students engage in a semester-long dialectic between theory and practice.

Citizen Alum
The brainchild of Julie Ellison (founding director emerita of Imagining America and faculty member at the University of Michigan), Citizen Alum reaches beyond the usual suspects concerned with community engagement in higher education by connecting development officers, student affairs professionals, and recent and more professionally seasoned alumni. While alumni often identify as "donors" or "sports fans," Citizen Alum expands the options for identification by connecting alumni at different phases of their lives and careers with students at different transition points within two-year and four-year institutions. With diverse campus teams conducting focused listening projects supported by a national learning community (of thirty institutions and growing), Citizen Alum builds ideas, practices, and campus cultures that support civic-minded students, alumni, faculty, staff, and other members of the community. Undergraduates enrolled in appropriate courses use a shared questionnaire with special emphasis on issues of citizen engagement to interview alumni. Through these interviews, students explore the magnitude and range of alumni's citizenship activities and also question interviewees about their postgraduate trajectories through the world of work. Ellison and her partners, including the Jandris Center for Innovative Higher Education at the University of Minnesota and Imagining America, are working together as agents of and allies in civic learning across the college-to-life range of life transitions including college and work. Citizen Alum heightens students' awareness of the multiple possible pathways for stimulating civic agency in professional contexts as well as the potential economic impact of civically engaged work.

Syracuse University Engagement Scholars
The Syracuse University Engagement Scholars program supports recent graduates for at least a year after graduation so they can develop careers as civic professionals in central New York State. Imagining America helps these scholars find jobs in

the region and facilitates monthly seminars about the ethics of civic work. Additionally, Syracuse University's deans provide scholarships covering tuition for graduate-level courses. Reflections from engagement scholars help punctuate the idea of the center of the civic. One student says, "It is a wonderful way to provide more visibility to the work of young graduates in the community and to encourage community members to invest their time and attention in relationships with campus partners."[8] Another concurs, describing the program as "one of the few ... that integrate students into the community, promoting inclusion at the same time. [It is v]ery beneficial to all who meet the students [and] provid[es] an excellent experiential opportunity to learn, grow, and bond with the CNY [central New York] community."[9] The Engagement Scholars program offers multiple pathways for stimulating a "civic professionalism" mindset among recent SU graduates from various degree programs, while also deepening these graduates' connections with the community around the institution in which they feel invested. The program model also foregrounds reciprocity in community–campus partnerships.

Engaged Undergraduate Research Group
Six IA institutions (Auburn University, Drew University, Macalester College, Millsaps College, Syracuse University, and the University of Miami) have collaborated to form the Engaged Undergraduate Research Group. Funded by the Teagle Foundation, this interinstitutional learning community and research project focuses on the development of "civic professionalism" as a roadmap for transforming educational practice through a dual focus on faculty work and student learning. Interweaving the traditional strengths of the liberal arts, the values of civic inquiry and reflection, and the practical work of sustaining and supporting our communities and ourselves, the research group allows each participating institution to pursue its own specific strategies for putting civic professionalism into action. Project participants experiment with pedagogical practices on multiple levels to engage with the organizational structures within departments and schools in order to impart to students a civically engaged, critical education integrating professional possibilities. Designed to connect with the curriculum, the cocurriculum, and other institutional structures that shape faculty work, the projects hold the potential to alter those structures to better accommodate and encourage engaged faculty work and, consequently, engaged student learning. Three of the participating campuses are focusing on building faculty capacity for integrating civic professionalism into the curricula and other structures.

The Northern Arizona University CRAFTS Project
An expansive movement supporting engaged democratic pedagogy at Northern Arizona University, CRAFTS (Community Reengagement for Arizona Families, Transitions, and Sustainability) is a compelling example of civic learning and teaching embedded in the core curriculum. Action Research Teams (ARTs) that have curricular connections with the First Year Seminar (FY Seminar) program are an integral part of this initiative. Professors Romand (Rom) Coles and Blase

Scarnati, key leaders of this university-wide effort, report that faculty members integrate ARTs into the curricula of about forty FY Seminar sections each year. Each course's emphasis emerges from "real world issues" identified and cultivated reciprocally with community and university partners, including sustainability, social justice, and grassroots democracy. Participating faculty, student affairs professionals, and community partners aspire to enhance the commonwealth by providing critical thinking and action skills to students as an essential component of the curriculum, helping students as citizens to reflect upon the multiple possible modes of democratic engagement. These efforts place the center of the curriculum at the center of the civic.

CONCLUSION: FIVE SENSES OF ENGAGEMENT

If the center of the civic is the ability to truly see and respond to the urgent needs of others, then I believe that there are senses, much like our human abilities to see, hear, touch, smell, and taste, that we need to develop as a means of fortifying civically engaged work. I have conceptualized these five "senses of engagement" as hope, history, passion, empathy, and planning, symbolized by the five fingers of the human hand.

The sense of *hope* (thumb) is critical and substantial, albeit sometimes abstract. Like regular hydration, it can be easily neglected but is always tremendously rejuvenating. Just as the opposable thumb greatly facilitates our human efforts to secure and command, this sense allows us to grab hold of dynamic principles and ideas that lead to action. In the face of seemingly intractable solutions, hope helps us initiate a powerful offensive to confront entrenched dysfunction. It is a kind of springboard that builds momentum.

Many in academe suffer from what I call the Ivory Tower mentality,[10] celebrating as an ideal their detachment from the larger community. I regard this mentality as one of the greatest challenges to higher education transformation. A sense of hope can mitigate the lull of the status quo and facilitate the creation of spaces for cultivating an ethos of expectation. For example, Craig Steven Wilder in his recent book *Ebony and Ivy: Race, Slavery, and the Troubled History of America's Universities* has demonstrated that most, if not all, of America's Ivy League universities played a significant role in the vile institution of slavery by drawing upon and leveraging resources from that enterprise to support their founding.[11] At the same time, American higher education institutions have played critical roles in moving our society toward democracy. The sense of hope helps us see that despite its troubling historical roots, American higher education can honor socially generated knowledge and engagement with community. Hope helps us navigate this tension between past and future and calls our greater civic selves to strengthen American democracy.

This hope should lead us to consider the critical importance of having a sense of *history* (pointer finger)—truly reckoning, with honesty and integrity, with the facts of social reality, regardless of how ugly they may be. A sense of history helps us find the roots of engagement in American higher education so that we can reconnect to these roots with neither nostalgia nor paralysis. The sense of history helps us become conscious of past decisions, commitments, and values so we can seize present and future opportunities lucidly, robustly, and purposefully.

The sense of *passion* (tall finger, *see page 76*) is like oil in the sputtering engine of hope, lubricating the pistons and bearings of engagement in ways that assist us in transcending the disappointments (as vile as they may be) of history. One of the most compelling aspects of higher education is the opportunity it provides to nurture the life of the mind, allowing life's animating questions to penetrate one's work. The sense of passion drives us toward and through long working hours and the development of complex theoretical constructs as we imagine innovative new possibilities grounded in, among, and beyond the disciplines. But passion often dissipates quickly and must be cultivated continually. It contains bite but lacks depth. To be truly useful, our sense of passion must

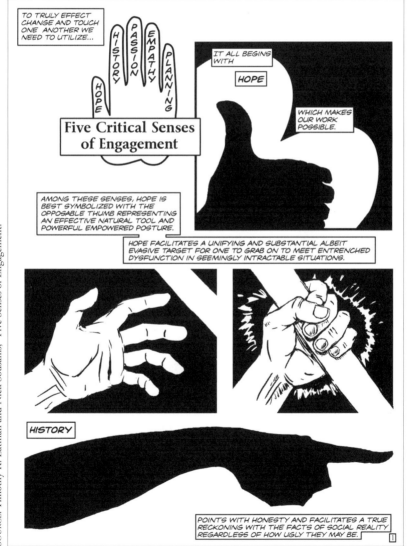

SOURCE: Timothy K. Eatman and Nick Sousanis, "Five Senses of Engagement."

lead to increasingly deeper understandings about one aspect of the center of the civic: empathy, which enables us to save each other in battle.

A sense of *empathy* (ring finger) makes us realize that we all have skin in the game; we are all connected. It is a force to help passion mature and evolve so its usefulness can be sustained. A sense of empathy helps us recognize our duty to maximize the opportunities academe presents so that it truly becomes a portal of ubiquitous possibilities rather than a sorting system or a dis-agentic institution dominated by flat discourses and models of knowledge.[12] A sense of empathy urges us to strive for full participation,[13] questioning how our colleges and universities can live up to the multifaceted needs of twenty-first-century life.

Full participation practices and thinking facilitate the creation of spaces where people, regardless of identity, background, or institutional position, can thrive and realize their gifts, talents, and capabilities.

The smallest finger serves as a reminder that we must attend vigilantly to the sense of *planning* (pinky). We must create iterative, detailed, deliberate, systematic, and contextually relevant plans that provide traction for steps toward progress. As researchers and scholars, we are well aware of the importance of systematic, structured inquiries and the rigor that it takes to sustain them. The sense of planning arises from the skill sets that thought leaders and intellectual harbingers develop. This planning is watered by hope, nourished by history, activated by passion, and solidified by empathy.

Like the physical human senses, the five senses of engagement are not manifest in everyone in the same ways. But just as the remaining senses become heightened when one physical sense fails or is not present, the five senses of engagement can complement and compensate for each other. It is very powerful to be part of a community that recognizes, celebrates, and leverages its members' diverse abilities. This awareness and compact can serve to enhance the civic context for all. The five senses of engagement may prove useful in our quest to sustain a focus on the center of the civic, both in and beyond our academic work.

NOTES

1. Timothy K. Eatman, "Making Scholarship Tangible: Syracuse University & Imagining America," *Kettering Foundation News* (Dayton, OH: The Kettering Foundation, 2012), http://kettering. org/kfnews/making-scholarship-tangible.

2. William Deresiewicz, "The Miseducation of America: The Movie 'Ivory Tower' and the Rhetoric of Crisis and Collapse," *The Chronicle of Higher Education*, June 19, 2014.

3. George D. Kuh, *High-Impact Educational Practices: What They Are, Who Has Access to Them, and Why They Matter* (Washington, DC: Association of American Colleges and Universities, 2008).

4. William M. Sullivan, "Markets vs. Professions: Value Added?" *Daedalus* 134, no. 3 (2005): 19–26.

5. Religious revivals were so common in central New York during the nineteenth century that the area became known as the "burned-over district," as it was said that no more souls were left to be converted.

6. Kevin Bott in Keith Kobland, "Imagining America: Art as Civic Engagement," *Syracuse University News* (Syracuse, NY: Syracuse University, 2012), http://news.syr.edu/imagining-america-art-as -civic-engagement.

7. I use the term "agentic" to signify agency or the ability to enact agency as related to communities, individuals, or groups.

8. Quote selected from non-published interviews with Syracuse University Engagement scholars as part of a fall 2013 program survey.

9. Ibid.

10. Though commonly used today, the term "Ivory Tower" can be found in early use in Charles Augustin Sainte-Beuve, *Pensées d'Août* [Thoughts of August] (Rue Christine: Eugene Renduel, 1837).

11. Craig Steven Wilder, *Ebony and Ivy: Race, Slavery, and the Troubled History of America's Universities* (New York: Bloomsbury Press, 2013).

12. See note 7. I use the term "dis-agentic" to indicate a lack of agency.

13. Susan Sturm, Timothy K. Eatman, John Saltmarsh, and Adam Bush, "Full Participation: Building the Architecture for Diversity and Public Engagement in Higher Education" (white paper, Center for Institutional and Social Change, Columbia University Law School, New York, 2011), http://www.umb.edu/editor_uploads/images/odi/Full_Participation_Catalyst_Paper_with_ acknowledgements_FINAL.pdf.

CONTRIBUTORS

Sybril Bennett is professor of journalism at Belmont University.

Dan Butin is associate professor and dean of the School of Education and Social Policy at Merrimack College and executive director of the Center for Engaged Democracy.

Christina P. Colon is assistant professor of biological sciences at City University of New York Kingsborough Community College.

Timothy K. Eatman is a professor of education at Syracuse University's School of Education and faculty codirector of Imagining America: Artists and Scholars in Public Life.

Ashley Finley is national evaluator for Bringing Theory to Practice and senior director of assessment and research at the Association of American Colleges and Universities.

Patricia Gurin is the Nancy Cantor Distinguished Professor Emerita of Psychology and Women's Studies at the University of Michigan.

Barbara Holland is affiliated professor at Portland State University and director of academic initiatives in social inclusion at the University of Sydney.

Carole Frances Lung is an assistant professor of fashion and textiles at California State University–Los Angeles

Biren A. (Ratnesh) Nagda is professor of social work and director of the Intergroup Dialogue, Education and Action (IDEA) Center at the University of Washington.

Seth Pollack is professor of service learning and director of the Service Learning Institute at California State University–Monterey Bay.

John Rowden is program director of Toyota TogetherGreen at the National Audubon Society.

Bringing Theory to Practice

Bringing Theory to Practice (BTtoP) is an independent project in partnership with the Association of American Colleges and Universities. It is supported by the S. Engelhard Center (whose major contributors include the Charles Engelhard Foundation and the Christian A. Johnson Endeavor Foundation, in addition to other foundations and individuals).

BTtoP encourages colleges and universities to assert their core purposes as educational institutions not only to advance learning and discovery, but also to advance both the potential and well-being of each student as a whole person and education as a public good that sustains a civic society.

BTtoP supports campus-based initiatives that demonstrate how uses of engaged forms of learning that actively involve students, both within and beyond the classroom, can contribute directly to their cognitive, emotional, and civic development. The work of the project is conducted primarily through sponsored research, conferences, grants to colleges and universities of all types, and publications—notably including *Transforming Undergraduate Education: Theory that Compels and Practices that Succeed,* edited by Donald W. Harward (Lanham, MD: Rowman & Littlefield, 2012.).

BTtoP provides a rare source of intellectual and practical assistance to all institutional constituencies that are seeking to make or strengthen the changes needed to realize their missions of learning and discovery, and that are working to create campus cultures for learning that recognize the necessary connections among higher learning, students well-being, and civic engagement.

Information about current grant opportunities, project publications, and forthcoming conferences is available online at **www.BTtoP.org**.